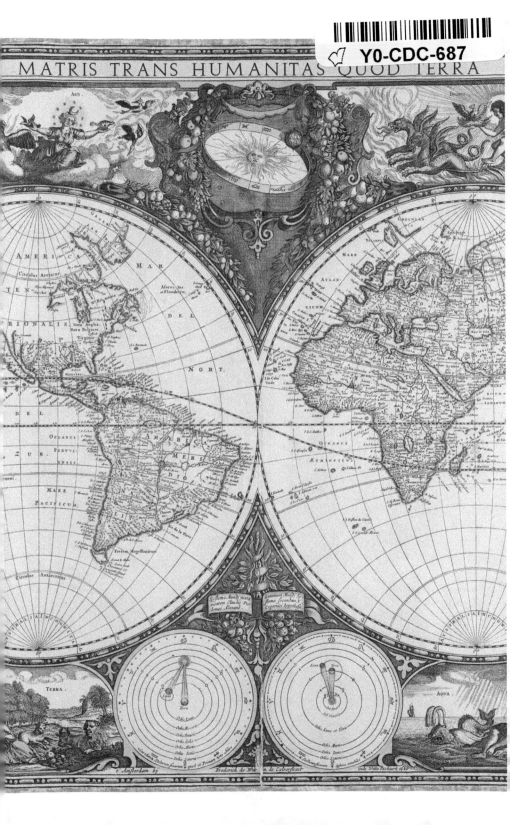

RL __8 - 9__

Call Me Okaasan

A D V A N C E   R E V I E W S

"In *Call Me Okaasan*, Suzanne Kamata and her troupe of gifted writers take us on a worldwide tour of motherhood across the cultures, each stop an unflinching look into one mother's efforts to shepherd her children through unfamiliar territory. Prepare to laugh, cringe, cry, and cheer on these women, and know that their poignant stories will stay with you long after you've turned the last page."

—Rebecca S. Ramsey, author of *French by Heart*

"Like everything Kamata has written and edited, this collection reveals to its readers new ways of seeing family, that always perplexing and intriguing concept." —mamazine.com

"Through immigration, adoption, blended-culture families— or simply temporary residence abroad—children can find themselves forced to bridge very different cultural and linguistic worlds. In this collection of well-written, honest and thought-provoking essays, parents reflect on the challenges of raising these global nomads, including concerns about prejudice, language skills, separation from extended family and friends, adapting (or not) to foreign childrearing practices, and their own feelings of guilt and doubt—but with ultimately positive conclusions about the value of their families' experiences."

— Patricia Linderman, Editor in Chief, Tales from a Small Planet, Co-author, *The Expert Expat: Your Guide to Successful Relocation Abroad*, www.expatguide.info

"Spans not only the width of the proverbial womb but also the width of the world. Each piece in this timely, lovingly honed collection has much to teach about parenting across cultural and cartographic lines. What I like most about the book is its ability to transition effortlessly between emotional personal confession, to clear-sighted global observation, and back again. *Call Me Okaasan* should be kept on the most accessible bookshelf. Mothers of all stripes will retrieve it often."

—Chandra Prasad, Originator and Editor, *Mixed: An Anthology of Short Fiction on the Multiracial Experience*

"The Earth-deep essays provided in this book help mothers the world over to remember their roots while celebrating motherhood from the mountains of Kyrgyzstan to the farm-lands of rural Japan. Motherhood, in any language, is deeply challenging. Doing so with transplanted roots adds a whole new layer of meaning to the experience. Bravo to these brave women for their honesty in showing a most truthful side to expat motherhood!"

—Christine Louise Hohlbaum, Author, *SAHM I Am: Tales from a Stay-at-Home Mom in Europe*

"The contributors to this lovely and almost lyrical anthology of mothering far from home, face all the regular roadblocks of raising healthy and happy children and then some. This collection will resonate with so many expatriate families or those who have chosen to live abroad. More importantly, buried in the narratives are many true gems of wisdom of cross-cultural mothering."

—Robin Pascoe, Expatriate Press Limited, Author, *Raising Global Nomads: Parenting Abroad in an On-Demand World*

MATRIS TRANS HUMANITAS QUOD TERRA

Call Me Okaasan
Adventures in Multicultural Mothering

Edited by Suzanne Kamata

Wyatt-MacKenzie Publishing
DEADWOOD, OREGON

Dedicated to Kavita and Louise

Call Me Okaasan

Call Me Okaasan
Adventures in Multicultural Mothering

Edited by Suzanne Kamata

Wyatt-MacKenzie Publishing, Inc.
DEADWOOD, OREGON

www.WyMacPublishing.com
(541) 964-3314

Requests for permission or further information should be addressed to:
Wyatt-MacKenzie Publishing, 15115 Highway 36,
Deadwood, Oregon 97430

CONTENTS

Call Me Okaasan: An Introduction
by Suzanne Kamata

"I'm America-sick," my nine-year-old son said one July afternoon as I was driving him home from school.

Huh? I was unsure of how to respond. Did he mean that he was sick of American culture, which was pervasive even in rural Japan? Perhaps he'd been watching too much "Hannah Montana" on cable TV. Or maybe he meant that he had a fever for all things from the United States. He actually *liked* Hannah Montana, or at least he'd told me several times that he did. But then he said, "I'm really looking forward to going to America next month." *Oh. I get it. He means "America-sick" as opposed to "homesick."*

Although my son and daughter are, by virtue of my nationality, American citizens, they have never lived in the United States, nor in any sort of international enclave. Their father is Japanese, making them citizens of this country as well, and they have been brought up surrounded by Japanese on the island of Shikoku. They go to Japanese schools, communicate via Japanese languages, and eat Japanese food. If pressed, I would have to say that they are more Japanese than American.

A few years ago, my son had emphatically declared himself Japanese. I'd felt personally rejected by this, but I figured it was better for him to have a strong Japanese identity than no identity at all. I'd read a great deal about the kind of confusion experienced by "third culture kids" and "global nomads." But I also worried that he would be bullied by his peers in the conservative farming community where we live—a place where even folks from the next town over are seen as vaguely foreign.

I enrolled him in a nearby private school boasting a curriculum in international English. Some of the students had lived abroad for a year or two, and a few had at least one foreign parent. Even better, half of the classes were taught in English. He seemed happy and comfortable there, and had become friends with the only other boy in his class with a Western mother and Japanese father. He'd begun to think of himself as American again.

While it pleases me to have a compatriot in the house, I have mixed feelings about my son's shifting alliances. Since I have no idea what I'm doing, no real clue as to how to raise a bicultural child, I can't help wondering if this America-sickness points to some kind of failure on my part. Perhaps he doesn't feel that he fits in at school. Perhaps he doesn't fit into Japan.

I don't always fit in so well either.

When I became a mother here in Japan, I carried certain assumptions. I would most definitely not sleep with my children at night, as most Japanese mothers did, and I would employ a babysitter once in a while so that my husband and I could spend quality time together, just the two of us, as most Japanese mothers did not. I expected that I would teach my children my mother tongue—English—and that I would nurture their American palates. I would introduce American holidays to them and I would have them call me "Mommy."

Of course nothing ever turns out according to plan. Sleeping in close proximity to our twins was easier than getting up several times a night to calm them down, and actually seemed quite sensible. And the babysitter I imagined? Well, in Japan, that role is usually the grandmother's, but my mother-in-law wasn't up to taking care of infant twins all by herself. My daughter, we discovered, was deaf, and since acquiring even one spoken language has proven to be very difficult for her, we decided to raise her using mainly Japanese sign language. As far as food goes, my son has developed an inconvenient taste for imported instant macaroni and cheese, but he and my daughter dislike many of my childhood favorites—banana bread, sweet pickles, and potato salad. And while I have gone to great efforts to duplicate an American Thanksgiving feast, complete with roasted turkey, cranberry sauce, cornbread, and pumpkin pie, the legendary meeting of the Pilgrims and Native Americans has little meaning for children raised in rural Japan. (And they're not too crazy about the cranberry sauce.)

I did succeed in getting my son to call me Mommy, when he was small, and now, Mom—at least most of the time. In front of Japanese friends, he calls me "Okaasan," as does most everyone else. During my first few years in Japan I was called "Sensei" or "Suzanne-sensei," due to my job as an English teacher. However, since having children, everyone, from my mother-in-law to my kids' teachers to door-to-door salesmen, calls me the Japanese name for mother. The only reason my husband doesn't call me "Okasaan" is because I asked him not to.

I don't think that I live up to the title "okaasan." I'm pretty useless when it comes to helping out with Japanese homework in this nation of "education mamas," and my son lingers at the bottom of his class. According to a memo sent home from my daughter's school, I shouldn't be feeding my children cold cereal for breakfast, *a la americaine*. Furthermore, the boxed lunches that I prepare for them are always wrong, somehow, and I make "mistakes" in the way that I dress them. I can never remember the official day for changing from long sleeves to short sleeves and vice versa. I don't make my children gargle with water after playing outdoors, as Japanese mothers do, in order to prevent sickness. What other Japanese mothers take for granted, comes to me after much trial and error. The rules for motherhood, it seems, are different here, and are sometimes at odds with my beliefs. Instead of thinking back to my own childhood or looking to the Japanese mothers around me for guidelines, I often feel the urge to consult with other mothers raising their children across cultures. Thus, this book was born.

Like me, the writers represented here are raising their children with an awareness of two or more cultures. Some mothers, such as Violeta Garcia-Mendoza and Angela Turzynski-Azimi, grew up in multicultural, bilingual households and have some idea of what's ahead.

Some of these women write of the anxiety that accompanies first-time motherhood. Saffia Farr, a British writer in Kyrgyzstan, for instance, wonders if she is endangering her unborn baby by seeking antenatal care in a developing country where the doctor's tools are not necessarily sterile. In "Like the Lotus," American Leza Lowitz worries that the Japanese toddler she and her husband adopt will be bullied because of his mother's nationality. Meanwhile, on the other side of the world, Susannah Elisabeth Pabot, an Austrian-American living in France remembers growing up in the shadow of her expatriate mother's despair. In her lyrical essay, "Eleven Snapshots for Your Baby Book, Reconstructed in Blues," she wonders, "How to become a mother without drowning in my own mother's sadness?"

Mothers also ask, "How to raise a child abroad in the mother tongue?" Language preoccupies many of us. While some bystanders believe that bicultural children absorb second languages effortlessly, these writers know that this is not the case. Devorah Lifshutz, who didn't understand her parents' Hungarian while growing up, vows in "Promises to Myself" that her Israeli-born children will learn English, and encounters a few hurdles along the way. Across the ocean, Corey Heller, a native-English speaker bucks tradition by choosing to speak German to her children in their Seattle home. And in Japan, novelist Holly Thompson's American children experience "Two Versions of Immersion," as they learn Japanese at school.

Several mothers write about their adjustments to their children's other cultures, such as Dee Thompson, a single mother who adopted an eleven-year-old from Russia. She takes a crash course in Russian culture and language in order to get along with her daughter. Meanwhile, Michele Corkery gets a lesson in multiculturalism at home when she enrolls her white daughter in a school in Boston's Chinatown and is forced to confront her feelings about her daughter's appropriation of African-American speech patterns. Some write of bafflement, such as Xujun Eberlein, the descendant of strong, Chinese women, who is dismayed by her teen-aged daughter's dismissal of her ancestors—and by her daughter's typical American behavior.

While mothering in a foreign country, or raising a child with a father from another culture, or learning about an adopted child's native culture, our lives are frequently enriched, our visions expanded. We experience new styles of celebrations and ceremonies, taste never before eaten foods, and learn new ways of thinking. Pondering the conditions of expatriate African mothers in South Africa, Canadian Katherine Barrett finds a connection to mothers all over the world. Whatever our conditions, she writes, we are all "carrying on despite politics and worry and irritation and self."

Finally, these writers remind us that our children are individuals and that although we may try to mold them, they have much to teach us. In the bittersweet "Adapting Back Home," Andrea Martins finds that her children adjust to her native Australia faster than she does, and that she cannot force them to retain Mexican culture. And as Marie Lamba writes in "The View from Outside," sometimes we can only observe from the sidelines as our children try to figure out what is expected of them. No matter how much we strive to influence our kids, it appears that they will ultimately work out issues of identity by themselves.

Throughout this journey, I suspect that we mothers—whether we're called *Okaasan, Mutti, Ummi* or something else—will be going through transformations of our own. As this book points out, however, we're all in this together, muddling through, carrying on.

Eleven Snapshots for Your Baby Book, Reconstructed in Blues
by Susannah Elisabeth Pabot

ONE
May, 1989. Graz, Austria.

A girl stands at a closed door. Long blond hair, lighter than yours, but the waves are the same. She raises her hand, knocks. Again, there is no answer. It is three in the afternoon, but she knows that behind this door she would find black darkness. Blinds lowered to cut out all daylight. Her mother sleeping in the day, waking at night. Living in the rhythm of another country. American time.

Before, there were enormous brown boxes flying over the Atlantic. Cheerios for this girl and her younger sister and brothers. Peanut butter to build an American world in this small Austrian town. Sesame Street videos. But the packages have stopped. The American grandfather gone. The last link. Darkness.

And something else happened. Something the girl can't understand. At night, her mother wakes, and there are screams. Entangled with her father's angry words. Sometimes the girl puts her head under her pillow. Sometimes she gets up and walks down the stairs. These are the nights she wants to forget.

Other nights, there is silence. Just a slice of light under her mother's locked door. When she is let into her mother's room there are pieces of paper scattered, open notebooks, ink pens on the floor.

"I'm writing honey. I've finally started to write. But it's ugly stuff. Don't touch it! Too ugly for anyone to read. I have to destroy it all."

The girl stays silent. Oh, Mama. Why? Come back. Don't hide. Live.

Please don't worry for this girl. She will fly to another country, where she can speak only English, her mother tongue. She will create a home for herself, in a city of foreigners. There, you will meet her. She will hold you.

TWO
Autumn 2004. London, England.

Here you are, just born. Days, weeks old. My arms encircle your body—a womb-shaped bundle, unbearably fragile—and I watch you cry.

The overwhelming fear of not loving, of not loving enough. Of not knowing how.

Your mouth opening and closing around my flesh. Pain and relief, too close together.

How to become a mother without drowning in my own mother's sadness?

THREE
December 2005. Paris, France.

You, fourteen months old, sitting naked on my stomach. Every day, for hours in warm, shallow water. In your *grand-mère's* windowless bathroom. I watch our skin grow wrinkles, watch you play with blue plastic boats, watch the red tap turn as I add more hot. Here we are safe. Another womb, this one is big enough for us both.

I don't think you understand this yet: we are not on a visit.

I don't ever want to step out into the cold again. We have left your first home—and I am not ready for anywhere else yet.

Your father calls from far away.

"You can't stay in there all day. *Mon amour.* Please."

I add still more hot water and you swim up to me through our soapy sea.

Beyond that peeling, gray wall, his childhood room fills with cardboard boxes—everything we own. Stacking one above the other, only a sliver of a window left uncovered. How much light is enough light? How much air? To breathe comfortably—to survive?

Your father's first gift to me, so long ago, in London: Flaubert's *Madame Bovary.* His voice reading aloud in his language.

Your hands reach out of the water, reach for my breast, my too-big baby. And holding my nipple tightly in your mouth with your teeth, you smile.

One tiny room for a whole family. Two mattresses on the floor. A door that refuses to close. Does it matter that this new city is called Paris?

Stop.

This urge to beautify, to write a splendid fiction for you, a pastel bedtime story. A song. A sweet dream. When you were still a baby, my darling, we moved to your Papa's home: Paris. It was Christmas-time. Garlands hung from trees along the *Champs Elysées*. *La Tour Eiffel* illuminated. Millions of sparkling lights reflected into the Seine. Into your blue eyes as I held you up whispering: "Look, honey, this is your city. This is where you will grow."

Baby books in soft colors anticipate these beautiful stories. Memories you won't long to forget. First half-smiles, cherub laughter. This is what we, mothers, are supposed to preserve, to annotate for you, our babies.

I never made a baby book for you. Bad mother. I didn't even try. No notes, no photos, not even home movies. Some digital images saved on our hard drive. Random jpegs sent by friends. Our families ask: why don't you ever send pictures?

Bad mother.

I was luckier; my mother made a baby book for me. A delicate bird on the cover, a pink ribbon in its beak. Pink for a baby girl, all sweetness and song. Inside, a tiny hospital bracelet with my brand-new name on it, a newspaper clipping in German announcing my birth, the strangeness of a two-dollar bill between two pages, dated the year I was born. A lock of baby hair. The image of your beautiful grandmother in a bed, holding me, half-looking at the camera, half-looking ahead—where to? Through the window at snow falling in Vienna?

The emptiness. The longing for truth. Always this longing to understand.

Maybe, my darling girl, *la Tour Eiffel* was illuminated. Maybe we did take you to see those brilliant lights. I know this for sure: around the corner from where your *grandmère* lives, down *rue Ménilmontant*, far in the distance that December I saw a tiny *Tour Eiffel* hiding in yellow-gray smog. The size of a plastic replica, sold by illegal immigrants out of plastic bags at its base.

Fragments in snapshots—for you. Scraps. Colors. Blues.

The blue of your eyes the day after you were born, looking up at me for the first time, our bodies separated by force—mine left forever scarred. That unbearably blue winter sky as we walk across Waterloo bridge, your breath warm, wet against my chest. Blue patterns in a white blanket, knit by your great-grandmother for my mother, trapped in the darkness of one of our boxes. My mother's blue dress the day she meets my father. The marks on her aging body changing color—blue-green, blue-yellow, blue-black—remembering her falls, her legs too weak to hold her after weeks, months, years in bed in a dark room, far, too far from her home.

Where to find a beginning, a starting point for this narrative? The impossible need to reconstruct, to spin back in time to an origin. To create a coherent structure, to make some sense—for you.

FOUR
July 1945. Wellfleet, Cape Cod.

A young woman sits in a chair by her window. Look!

You have her nose, the same length, that gentle downward curve at the end. We recognized this nose at your twenty-week ultrasound exam—blurry, gray dots on a screen telling the history of your genes. The wonder of biology.

White wool in her hands and threads of blue. Her hands are beautiful, they are hers and my mother's and mine and yours. Long silver needles dancing.

Next to the young woman, a newborn lying in her cradle. The baby breathes the salt air from the Atlantic and her lips move—my mother, smiling. By the window, a 'Rose of Sharon' blooms. Deep purple-blue blossoms, planted for this American girl born on a summer day. By her immigrant father, in celebration.

Suddenly—the telephone rings. The young woman reaches forward, picks up the receiver, turns it toward her ear.

"Yes, hello?"

The sound of her voice—and her baby smiles again. Unnoticed.

"Mum. Steve is outside. I can't talk for long."

Silence. The young woman lets the receiver fall onto her shoulder, gazes out of the window. A cardinal lands in the Rose of Sharon, tilts its head toward her. For a moment, she forgets the voice talking into the cloth of her blue dress, drenched in tears.

"*Clarice, come back here with the children. He's not good enough for you.*"

A whisper: "I love him, mum."

Far away, the girl-baby's screams, the fingers of her tiny hands out-stretched, empty.

A large man moves into the frame. He lifts his hand, leans into the door-frame. His dark hair light, covered in wood-dust, blue paint on his pants.

"Clarice?"

Your hand, my hand—hers, covering the receiver.

"It's mum."

"Tell her to let us alone. Please."

My grandmother shakes her head. "I can't."

"Then I will. Once and for all."

Footsteps across the room. Toward my mother's screams. A heavy hand tearing the receiver away from my grandmother's chest, shoving it into its cradle. Touching her cheek.

"For us, Clarice. She won't let us alone. Ever."

Always to feel different. Never completely accepted. The immigrant. *Die Amerikanerin. L'étrangére.*

His young parents stepping off a boat onto Ellis Island. Leaving behind—everything but each other. Sixteen babies later, in heavily-accented English mixed with Slovakian words—never forgotten, to die in poverty. And one of their sons marries a New England girl. The daughter of a doctor, the first man on the Cape to own a car. A miracle assembled out of a box, whole towns watching.

The baby's screams closer now—her mother at last reaches into the cradle. And the wool in her lap falls onto the floor, needles slipping out, a morning's labor unraveling.

FIVE

August 1965. In a train between Vienna and Bratislava. Central Europe.

A young student crosses her legs. Their shape is perfect, and she knows this. She wears a short blue dress. She is twenty years old. She doesn't have your nose, but she has your hands. They lie in her lap. She tries not to watch the Austrian boy in front of her, his eyes on the space where her thighs meet. Tries not to laugh out loud. Seventeen, eighteen, maybe, he reminds her of James Dean in her favorite movie: *East of Eden*. She turns her head and watches the landscape glide by. Flat, green fields. Vineyards. Scattered fir trees and blue sky. So unlike the mountains she expected. Soon this train will take her beyond the Iron Curtain into the land her grandparents left behind when they were her age—Slovakia. She feels the boy's gaze on her face and her hand reaches into her bag, pulls out a bar of dark chocolate. In an act of uncharacteristic courage, she leans forward, breaks off a row. Offers.

He smiles and his body moves toward hers.

When he will begin to stop loving her, more than twenty years later, she will still be far from her home. With nothing of her own in his country but his love.

Never to let love matter this much. Never to make the same mistake. To live. To want to stay alive.

On the same page of my open thesaurus: misery, misfit, misguided, mismatched, misplaced, miss, mistake.

In America she was brilliant. So clever and a beauty—everyone said.

SIX
May 2001. London.
Your father, before he became your father. Standing in

front of me in Hampstead Heath Tube Station—the deepest in London. In this city of foreigners I have fallen in love with a foreigner. We are trying to say goodbye. I know he is unhappy here, and I love him. I want him to be happy. I know he needs to go home. One last time, he asks me to come with him, but I answer no.

"I can't. I'm sorry. My love."

He stands in front of me until he cannot wait any longer without missing his train to Paris. He picks up his suitcases, taking everything that is his, leaving nothing in London but me.

He stands in the elevator. Its doors stay open for an eternity, make us see what could be possible but is not. Not yet. No, we don't imagine you yet. Silver doors close, sliding him out of my reach.

The pulling apart. The feeling of one's limb tearing off. The inability to regain balance, one-sided.

Walking back through London—alone. *Never to let love matter this much.* In my attic room on Lyndhurst Crescent I play the music he gave me: "No More Shall We Part." Nick Cave.

And all of those birds would've sung to
your beautiful heart
Anyhow

We managed five months—and he came back.

Tu vas, et tu viens. Je vais, et je viens. Et je te rejoins. Jane Birkin and Serge Gainsbourg. *Français.* English. Her light ethereal voice. When did they come apart? Why? And what did he die of?

Too much alcohol. Of course.

SEVEN
January 2006. Paris.

In the winter Paris is countless shades of gray, and I can't tell them apart. That first winter, endless rain, more than ever fell in London. And none of the snow of my Austrian childhood, not a single flake.

I add more hot water. Your father walks past the bathroom door, forgets we are inside, turns off the light. Darkness. My nipple in your mouth, you aren't frightened, your hands reach up to touch my face.

Yes, honey—I'm still here.

In my thesaurus, page 582, first entry:

misery (noun) unhappiness, distress, wretchedness, suffering, anguish, anxiety, angst, torment, pain, grief, heartache, heartbreak, despair, despondency, depression, desolation, gloom, melancholy, melancholia, woe, sadness, sorrow; informal: the dumps, the blues; literary: dolor. ANTONYMS contentment, pleasure.

After your birth: my job given up, his lost. The unraveling of one word: "redundancy." And his question, again: "Will you come with me to Paris? *Mon amour.*" How to say no with you in my arms? How to say yes?

Everything becoming smaller, tighter—no light, no air. And one gray afternoon: I scream. I hit my wrist against the wall, again and again; I stop only when the swelling has already begun. The pain catches up later, much later, in a French emergency room. Trying to explain myself. In red, blue, purple, black.

Unforgettable: your eyes, enormous holes, your arms, clinging to me. Silent screams I recognize: what is Mama doing?

I'm staying alive, honey. I am dancing against this wall, dancing for light, color.

Forgive me.

That night, through the crack above our boxes I find the dark-blue sky. Next to me on your little mattress, you stir. Your hand reaches for mine. Above us, I think, are the same stars, everywhere in our world. The very same constellations.

EIGHT
September 1968. Route 6, Cape Cod.

An alternative beginning. Another explanation. A family in a car, driving to a pizza restaurant in the fog. A father, a mother, a grown-up daughter, her Austrian boyfriend on his first visit to America. It was the daughter's idea to go out to eat so that her tired mother wouldn't have to cook another meal. She is happy; she wants her mother to be too. At least for one evening.

Fog on route 6. Low visibility. The father drives slowly, maybe too slowly.

"Angst" being in its origin a German word. *Auf Deutsch* meaning "fear." Ordinary, everyday fear. *Ich habe Angst for Spinnen*, for example. How close are misery and fear?

In the apartment building where your *grand-mère* lives, we take the elevator down to the garage. The stench of urine, and a stained piece of paper taped on the garage wall, reading: *C'est un garage, pas des toilettes. Est-ce que vous pissez contre le mur dans votre séjour?*

Your *grand-mère* drives the smallest car I have ever sat in, a white two-door Peugeot 106. In its back seat my knees rise at awkward angles toward my chin. We wind through Parisian traffic. I watch your father's head move as he speaks to his mother in French too fast for me to understand. They laugh. French outside the car, French everywhere. You fall asleep next to me, holding my hand and your hand drops out of mine.

Like my mother, always doubting my ability to write in a foreign country. *Boulangerie. Soldes. Avenue Gambetta.* Fearing losing my language surrounded by foreign words, I arm myself with dictionaries, thesauruses: life jackets, buoys.

How to find words to describe my grandmother Clarice's death. A neck—broken. The Austrian boyfriend— who will one day become your grandfather—sitting where I sit in the Peugeot, behind her in the back seat, witness to her last moment. In the last split-second he saw the other car driving into them in that late summer fog. He thought it would be him, but my grandfather was driving too slowly. It hit her and he was spared.

Survivors, the daughter and her Austrian boyfriend cling to each other. And she follows him to his country. She leaves behind her home, her broken father—and a future opening: on her desk, the day after the accident, an acceptance letter. Graduate studies, the promise of an academic career.

In Austria, her world narrows: foreign degrees are not accepted. Instead, four children are born. Some happiness, until they begin to grow up, away toward the outside world. And it is my father who becomes the academic, the published writer, the distinguished professor.

NINE
August 2004. London.

You, inside me. Swollen. I don't know it yet, but it is more than just the heat. We are both sick—my body failing you. As if anticipating that your ripening will be cut short, I bend over my sink preparing early. I wash your white and blue blanket—carefully, by hand—to lay it over your first bed outside me.

My mother's blanket, my blanket—now yours.

"Ready?" Your father's hands on my shoulders. We climb the steps of a red London bus. A Hopper retrospective in the Tate Modern. We don't know that this will be the last time I will leave home before the hospital. The bus sways, stops. A typical London scene unfolding: in the road before us a naked man, screaming. Police holding him down, hands desperately trying to cover himself. He looks up and for an instant his eyes—lost in another world—find mine.

At the Tate my head spins. I can barely stand. A canvas: *Cape Cod Morning*. A young woman by a window, looking out. No, leaning, reaching toward the outside world, toward the sunlight streaming in from the blue sky. Is she trapped?

Blue, my favorite color. Blue sky. Green-blue, purple-blue, dark blue. Monet's blues in the *Musée d'Orsay*. Picasso's blues. Cerulean. Ultramarine, aquamarine. Baby blue. I may have called you Indigo, but in the neonatal intensive care unit we decided you were golden. Our Aurélia Skye.

TEN

June 2005. Graz, Austria.

Emptiness in her forever dark room. A bed. Dirty sheets—she hardly ever washes them anymore, nor the few items of clothing she wears. His shirts, mostly. All the energy it takes to wash even herself, to make her legs bear her from her room to the bath, to lift her leg over the side, to step in.

What color is your misery, Mama? I've never asked you. Is it blue? Or is it colorless, the black darkness of your room, the night you so stubbornly prefer to day?

My mother's face isn't hers anymore. It's swollen up, like a moon. I'm afraid of that face, every time I see it. I want to look into it and say: "Where's my Mama?"

"It's all the drink," my sister says.

"It's those tablets she takes," my brother whispers.

"It's because your mother can't pull herself together," my father shouts.

I don't say anything. I live too far away. I ran, as far as I could, a long time ago, when my mother's face was still hers. Only the tear marks were already there on her cheeks, little paths pointing the way to what lay ahead.

I don't come back often.

But today I am here for a special reason: I am holding you. Your sleeping head lies on my breast. I've brought you to my childhood home for the first time. You are seven months old.

When I finally knock, she opens. Her eyes—in another

world—meet mine. And she cries out, waking you up. I expect you to scream, but you don't. You open your eyes, slowly, and you look into my mother's moon face.

It's not what I hoped for, not what she hoped for, either. Stop.

I'm a child again, two years old. I am with my mother. She is so beautiful. But her eyes are closed. I pull at her eyelashes, trying to open her lids with my small fingers. I don't think I am gentle. I'm worried: "Mama, where are you? Are you there, Mama?"

Mama, where are you?

Mama, where am I?

Your father asks me to come with him to Paris, and I say no. At first I say no.

"Light!" I cry out. *La lumière, mon amour. Je t'en prie: la lumière!*

ELEVEN
Late April 2006. Paris.

Suddenly, the trees on your *grand-mère's* street are in bloom. Bright pink blossoms. She says they will last one week, maybe two. It depends on the wind, and the rain. But suddenly there isn't any rain, and the blossoms stay much longer. Together, we walk beneath all this pink—a bride and a flower girl. I lift you up but they are too high to touch so you wave, your hand opens and closes.

Hello blossoms.

Hello spring.

I take you down *rue Ménilmontant*, we climb a bus, ride

to the *Jardin du Luxembourg*. In celebration. Under the trees, by the statues of the queens of France, you squat and play with the dusty pebbles. You throw one after the other through an iron grate. You listen to the sound of their fall. And your clothes turn a soft yellow-gray.

In a tree between two stone queens, a sculptor installs his *oeuvre*: a gigantic, silver-wire web, part of an open air exhibition held here every year. Next year under this tree— we don't know it yet—there will be an enormous, golden head. Smiling.

Today, you toddle over to the web. The artist, an old man, grins at the child. He bends down to your height. "*Regarde, il y a une araignée dans l'arbre,*" he whispers. His voice gentle, mischievous, taking pleasure in his creation. "*Bientôt, si tu restes, si tu regardes, elle va descendre. Elle va danser dans son nid.*"

But you are not frightened easily. You wait.

And through the trees, a woman approaches. So tall, so slim, so graceful—perfect in her imperfection. She comes closer and I recognize her: Charlotte Gainsbourg. Jane and Serge's daughter. Part English, part *française*. She doesn't see us, she is walking toward her children swinging on the green boat swings, and her mother, pushing them. Jane, old, still achingly beautiful. Watching her, for the first time I think: will I too be old here one day? Will I push your children on those swings?

Dr. Bucket in Bishkek
by Saffia Farr

I never imagined I would experience my first pregnancy in Kyrgyzstan. But why would I? I'd never even heard of Kyrgyzstan.

My husband Matthew is an international water consultant working on aid projects. After two years in southern Egypt he was posted to Kyrgyzstan, his project the valuable task of piping clean drinking water to remote villages. I was fifteen weeks pregnant and anxious about experiencing the new mysteries of my swelling body in an unknown land far from modern health care.

Kyrgyzstan is a former Soviet Republic. We arrived at four a.m. in the rain and found a grey city dominated by huge concrete tenement blocks, imposing institutions stamped with hammers and sickles and Lenin on a plinth in the center of a vast square. We were deposited in a cold, sparse flat with an unhygienic padded seat on the lavatory and only dry bread and cheese in the fridge. Lying on my hard, narrow bed I tried not to let my worries spiral into panic about whether I was endangering my unborn child by being there.

My first few weeks in Bishkek were dominated by my obsession with finding a doctor who spoke English. At that stage I didn't speak any Russian and was reluctant to play

Chinese whispers through a translator about intimate bodily functions. Anxious about my inexperience of pregnancy, I longed for medical reassurance, something I wasn't convinced I was going to find in Kyrgyzstan where hospitals haven't been updated since the Soviets first built them in the 1960s.

I'd not had much luck finding care in my nomadic pregnancy. I'd started in Copenhagen, Denmark, headquarters of the company Matthew worked for. There the Danish doctor had been more concerned about how I'd pay for my healthcare than discussing my debilitating headaches. My midwife in England had made me panic about all the checks and tests I wouldn't be able to have and was blatantly disapproving of me going to a country she'd never heard of. I'd felt completely abandoned.

On meeting people in a new country it's normal to swap banal comments about where you've lived and what job you or your partner does that causes you to travel. Preoccupied with my quest for a doctor I surprised everyone by skipping the pleasantries and immediately asking if they knew of anyone who could help. Most answers were disheartening: there were Canadian doctors in town, but they were only there to treat the miners who worked for a Canadian gold mining company; there was a good doctor at the American airbase, but she would only see employees of the American embassy. Everyone seemed to be in agreement that clinics in Bishkek had a dubious reputation. I became so desperate that I resorted to accosting a stranger with a baby in a supermarket to ask her where she'd had her antenatal care. My first piece of luck: she was English and took me to

Doctor "Bucket" who operated the only ultrasound machine in Bishkek.

Doctor Bucket worked at the "Rotdorm Hospital Number Three." He had spiky black hair, wore a turquoise lab coat and conducted his examinations with a cigarette behind his ear. I lay on a wooden bench while Bucket explored previously unseen cavities of my body with the transducer. He turned the screen towards me but disappointingly I could see only shadows: This was my baby but I wouldn't have believed it unless primed.

As Bucket spoke little English and I spoke limited Russian and no Kyrgyz, his diagnosis was a double thumbs up—not the comprehensive diagnosis I'd been hoping for but a positive start at least. I didn't learn details of its heart or whether the lungs were an appropriate size but I did discover the sex of baby; something we'd not wanted to know. I'd thought the examination was over and was trying to roll inelegantly off the bench when Bucket pushed me back down, prompted by a question from the assistant ticking boxes on my form. He wiggled the transducer and squinted.

"Penis, scrotum." Seemingly his only words of English.

"That'll be a boy then," I said to a surprised Matthew.

In the West pregnant women are harangued by books and magazines about what they should eat to maintain appropriate levels of folic acid, iron and essential nutrients for growth. My diet became another area of concern for me because although a capital city, Bishkek is not a commercial center. Most produce on sale is locally grown and seasonal, a form of provision I'd welcome and admire if I wasn't pregnant in country where staple foods were mutton fat and fermented mare's milk.

When we arrived it was the end of winter and there was little variety of fruit and vegetables: fortunately I like cabbage and beetroot but it can become rather repetitive. The pregnancy books I foolishly referred to recommended leafy greens, oily fish, oranges and avocados, none of which were available. I spent hours searching bazaars for spinach, wondering whether I was mad or irresponsible. In deciding to move to Bishkek I'd balanced risk and love. I wanted to be with Matthew at this momentous time of our lives, but not to the detriment of our child. I'd concluded that it wasn't necessarily healthy to sit at my parents' house just in case my blood pressure went up.

I was however fortunate enough to receive some ante-natal care. I found an English speaking doctor working in a training clinic on a US-sponsored program to improve the knowledge and skills of doctors. I became a living experiment and my check-ups involved five students standing around my prone body poking my swollen ankles and trying to measure my tummy. While a nervous girl prodded my belly with a wooden instrument trying to find a heartbeat, the doctor told me that medicine in Kyrgyzstan was at the level England reached in the Fifties, mixed with local superstitions and remedies involving onions and vodka. This didn't reassure me.

We take so much for granted in our modern world—basics such as running water and sanitation. I no longer take the pregnancy urine test for granted. In England it takes two minutes—a paper tester is dipped into a little pot and fades into a rainbow of purple, green or blue. In Bishkek it takes two hours. I sat on a wooden bench, queuing with ladies clutching liter vodka bottles containing their samples. The work of the technician looked like a science experiment; putting wee in test tubes, spinning them in a mini Ferris wheel then placing droplets on slides and examining them through a microscope. Unfortunately after all this effort I was still no wiser about mine and baby's health—the results were given in carefully enunciated Russian and I had no idea what she was talking about.

Language was not so much of a barrier as an insurmountable mountain. I am ashamed to admit that despite lessons, my grasp of Russian, the language used by most people in Bishkek, was slow. This made even the simplest daily task complicated; going to the doctor was a game of chance. On my first visit to the training clinic I'd been registered. This involved filling in a form. The first part was simple; a patient assistant pointed to equipment so I knew what to do—I stood on the scales, held out my arm for the blood pressure wrap and opened my mouth for a disposable thermometer. The next stage was trickier as it involved incomprehensibly long Russian sentences ending in questions. I shrugged and smiled apologetically and answered "no" to each query as the safest option. My admissions form probably included some peculiar information.

My inability to communicate was regularly frustrating. In one circumstance it became frightening. As part of my treatment I was sent for a routine blood test. I sat dutifully at a desk where a lady in a dirty lab coat was dipping a long pipette into a row of test tubes, their tops broken into viciously jagged peaks. Although she sometimes put the pipette in a jar of clear solution I wasn't convinced this was sterile or hygienic and was just trying to work out how to make my excuses and leave when she grabbed my wrist and pinned it to the table. With the other hand she jabbed at my index finger with what looked like a broken razor blade.

"What did you use to cut me?" I asked in English.

"Eh?" She was busy spattering my blood onto a slide.

"That metal, was it clean or did you use it for the person before?" She'd simply placed it on the table as if ready to use again. My voice was becoming shrill with panic as I imagined all the life threatening diseases my baby and I could have contracted. The woman had no idea what I was concerned about and looked bemused by the ranting foreigner.

"WAS-THE-METAL-STERILE?" Even slow, emphasized shouting didn't work. I ran out of the hospital to our flat where Matthew tried to calm my hyperventilating and make sense of what had happened.

We returned to the hospital in the hope of answers. My English speaking doctor was away but a man hidden away in a windowless office assured me that all practices were completely sanitary and I had nothing to fear. I wanted to believe him but was haunted by the image of the piece of metal lifted from the table rather than being snapped out of a sterile packet. I was not completely reassured until I'd had results of an HIV test back home.

After such an experience it might be natural to assume that I was glad to come home to England and that I ensured

I started my next pregnancy within safe reach of the English NHS. Actually, the reverse happened. Once I'd become accustomed to my unusual antenatal care I realized that I was very healthy. There wasn't the temptation of fast or processed food and as we entered spring the streets were full of stalls selling an abundance of cheap and fresh fruit and vegetables. Away from the obsessive commercialism of the West I was more relaxed. I didn't worry about whether I'd bought the best nipple cream or packed the correct things into my hospital bag because without the constant bombardment of all the things you must have for a good pregnancy, I just followed my instincts and let my body take control.

In fact, I became so calm about being a nomadic mother that I ended up starting my second pregnancy in Kyrgyzstan. Now I'm pregnant for the third time, in England, I miss the eccentricities of the students and being able to buy a kilogram of strawberries for twenty pence—although I do enjoy the speed and efficiency of a Western urine test!

Two Names for Every Beautiful Thing
by Violeta Garcia-Mendoza

One day, my son and daughters will ask me what I remember of Spain and I will talk about my garden. I will say that when I was a girl, the place I loved most in the world was *el jardin,* that this was the place I went while my Spanish father and my American mother built a house that crumbled. I will tell about the "u" of stone walls surrounding it, of how they were covered in thick strands of ivy that made them seem ancient, enchanted, as if they had been taken from a castle; about the honeysuckle spilling over the fourth wall of ceramic-tiled *terraza.* I will speak of the way the wind wrinkled the water over the blue and white swimming pool tiles, of the sound the *pomelos* made as they struck the ground like golden fists. I will tell about my solitary games, how I plucked geranium and rose petals off of their flowers and soaked them in water. How I watched, by night, trails of light form as the snails licked the walls with their slug bodies.

I will tell them that in this very place, their *mami* learned magic: to press my ear to the ground while sounds and words in Spanish and English ran through open doors, over the walls, to me. That *aqui, mami* learned to speak the two names for every beautiful thing.

I will not tell them this magic of mine was conditional,

that it granted itself to me only by virtue of my always existing in more than one place, simultaneously: Spain, the US, memory, the present tense. The subjunctive mood. More than likely, I will not need to; my three Guatemalan-born, Spanish- and Mayan-blooded, American-raised children will understand that part of the story already.

Before we adopted our children, I dreamt about their first mothers. Without having met them, I dreamt of meeting them and of seeing the way they manifested themselves in the children between us. I dreamt of making them the impossibly great promise to honor the lives they were giving my husband and I. In the dreams, recurrently, I promised to do this by love and by language.

My husband and I knew when we said our first yes to each of our children—that yes of *we choose you, we're waiting for you, come home*—that our children would inevitably lose certain people and things even as they gained us, and others. Our plan, our hope, was that we would try to ensure that their losses be as few as possible. And so, with a purpose that might not have been so fervent had our children come to us through birth, we set about fusing the American, the Spanish, the Guatemalan, flavors of our family.

For us, carrying this out has been more natural than the average person might expect. I speak more Spanish than English to the kids while my husband speaks more English than Spanish to them; but we both speak both. Most of the resources we have to think about—toys, books, music, media- go towards strengthening Spanish, while everything else over the course of the day falls into English.

And it's also less ordinary.

One mid-summer morning, a friend and I are walking our children in their strollers down the street. A woman stops us as we're walking, wanting to see the kids. She peeks into my friend's stroller, then bends over mine, extending a hand to my two year old son and daughter. They're engrossed in the local wildlife, watching a squirrel scamper across the street. My daughter yells *"Ardilla!"* and neither she nor her brother pay any attention to the stranger in front of them. When they don't take her hand, the woman asks them to at least say hello. When they don't do that either, she grows insistent.

"Don't they understand English? Don't they talk yet?" There's rising outrage in her voice.

My friend's son and daughter are a few months older than our kids. They're also fairer skinned, lighter eyed. Though she's a stranger, their mother is assumed to be American, which she is, whereas I am suspected in the neighborhood as a foreigner. It's not a coincidence that though it's my friend's children that actually sit in greater silence, their language development goes unquestioned.

This seems like the never-ending story of my kids' toddlerhood. Strangers, as well as some friends and extended family, ask whether they don't speak or understand English, whether their language skills are delayed, whether I'm confusing them by exposing them to two languages. It's not everyone that does this, and it's probably the same percent of the general population that accosts mothers everywhere to give unsolicited commentary on their children. Nevertheless, it catches at me, makes me wonder whether I'm burdening our kids with one more thing to make them unusual. And yet, this is not a wonder that makes me turn to Google, or to a parenting book, or to the pediatrician, for advice. Nor is it a wonder that will make me keep my voice down when I speak Spanish to the kids in public or train them to answer certain people in a certain way. It's a wonder that makes me keep on doing what I'm doing with the tug of instinct and personal memory.

When I speak to someone who knows both English and Spanish, often even my posture will change. The way I uncoil as surprising and restorative as a sigh. My husband points this out one evening as we sit on the terrace outside, after having just witnessed an animated forty-five minute phone call to my American, but equally bilingual, mother on the neighborhood drama (conducted in our familial brand of Spanglish, so as not to be overheard by others and understood). His jaw is set in a strong, handsome line, as always, but his eyes are uncertain about whether he should bring this up. I don't mind. I want him to be able to make sense of why my hands flutter expressively, and I hold my mouth differently, and my breath changes like this sometimes.

"When I'm around other bilingual people," I tell him, "there's no more 'either/or'. There's nothing I need to stress about not including. It's the gift of *and*. I get to speak and act the way my mind thinks."

He puts his arms around me. "*Nuestros niños tambien.*" Our kids, too.

One day, my son and daughters will tell me what they remember of their childhoods. They will not need to reconcile themselves with that half language of translation, but be full of that bilingual, bicultural magic of being able to go and come back constantly between place and time. They will speak of things my husband and I will know. Of the way, in Guatemala, the ground moved a bit beneath their still-small feet due to the volcanic soil. Of how, during rainy season afternoons, rain spilled from the great clouds over the city and thunder rumbled *entre las montañas,* making them stir. Of how, when we first met them, we whispered their names and tipped them from our arms towards tropical flowers. Of how they reached their small fingers towards the mosaics and the ceramic statues hung on the stucco walls of our Guatemalan friends' *patio.* They will tell us, maybe, of the way, in their memory's first *jardin,* the vines linked each plant to each other, like a thin, green thread of cobweb. Of the way they later noticed this can happen in Guatemala City, Madrid, Pittsburgh…anywhere. Listening to them, I suspect they'll remember more than I even expect. The breadth of their lives will astound me, even as I stand beside them.

One day. If I give them anything, may it be the chance to call forth all the beautiful things they deserve.

Like the Lotus
by Leza Lowitz

December 29, 2006.

I am standing on a cliff fifty feet above the Japan Sea, balanced on a precipice between two oceans. I don't know how life has brought me to this place, this beautiful rock on the Northern Izu Peninsula on the island of Honshu. But I'm here, with my husband and dog. We've hiked up twenty miles to stand on this small point of rock in Dogashima, watching the waves crest below and the falcons crest above.

It's my birthday; the dawn of a new year. I sit down on this line of solid land that cuts into the cliff and give thanks to all of those who have held my hand to pull me up the mountain of life. I feel safe, yet I am literally perched on a dangerous place, a narrow cliff that juts straight down to the ocean. But it's not the literal I am interested in. Deep in my heart, I feel a sense of security and peace that I've never felt before. So I shift my weight to one foot. I lift the other foot up, place it onto my thigh. I look straight ahead and hold my focus. If I look down I will be overcome with fear. I hold my tree pose, breathing deeply. Strength and courage flood my cells. I repeat my mantra: "I am calm, I am poised…at the center of life's storms, I stand serene."

It's taken me forty-four years to get here.

I've searched half the world for this feeling.

And I know, of course, that it is fleeting.

I don't have a Zen master, a guru, or even, really, a religion. But neither did Tu Fu, Basho, Musashi Miyamoto or countless other poets and wanderers who made their way through hills and valleys, over mountains and rivers, to seek solace. They didn't have to sit in a meditation hall and stare at a wall to look inside. They just looked around and paid attention to what was near them. Their teachers *were* the mountains, rivers, rocks, and trees. Their parents were Mother earth, Father sky. Then they woke up. Or should I say, were *awakened*. I'm waiting for my epiphany. I've found ten thousand other ways to be a mother, but I'm still waiting for a child.

Elegy

I have a friend who took his three-year-old boy up to the mountains in the Japanese countryside. The boy ran ahead excitedly, as little boys will do. There was a wooden footbridge. It hung over a steep ravine, a hundred foot drop. The boy ran ahead onto the footbridge. The footbridge was made of planks of old wood. Not many people walked in the mountains anymore. There were gaps in the planks. Big gaps.

The father watched.

Every year on the day the boy died, my friend posts a memorial picture of his son on his blog. The boy playing a drum set. Standing in front of a samurai helmet. Smiling for the camera. Making the peace sign with both hands. No words, no commentary. Only his son's picture and the word "elegy."

To remember. To honor.

Life is not safe. I know that. Nothing is certain. Things we hope for, dream about, come or don't come, and then are gone.

I meet with my friend often. In our own ways, we both mourn our lost children.

Somehow, we have been drawn together in this strange world to mirror each other's pain. To give each other comfort and hope. We *will* move on, our mutual presence seems to say. We give each other that.

Heartlines

My husband is *chonan*. In Japan, this is a serious business. Chonan means the oldest son and heir to the family name and whatever fortune it may have acquired. While we'd been "away" in the paradise of Northern California for ten years, his younger sister had been doing the dad's cooking and laundry. But his sister, now in her thirties, wanted to start her own life—open her own business, move on. We couldn't ask her to take care of the dad forever. It was Shogo's turn—our turn.

I hadn't wanted to go back to Tokyo, the busy life, the pollution, the stress. But I loved my husband, and wanted to be with him. And I knew that a good marriage was based on compromise—even sacrifice. After all, the root of the word sacrifice is *sacred*. In the highest sense, to sacrifice is to do something completely for someone else, with no personal gain. As an independent American woman, that took some getting used to.

And it was time to start a family.

I'd gone about trying to have a child the way I'd gone about everything else in my life—one part perseverance, one part "trusting the process." And I thought, as many do, that "if it's meant to be, it will be." I had a full, fantastic life and no regrets. But after eight years, I did something I'd never done before in quite the same way. I got down on my knees and prayed.

And then my beloved aunt got cancer. Her one regret is that she did not have children. She worked all her life in child protective services, and had wanted to adopt. She urges me forward with a force and conviction that only impending death can render.

I learn of an Australian psychologist who has adopted an infant in Japan. When I contact her, she gives me the name of the government agency—Jido Sodan Jo. The application asks questions like: why do you want a child, what kind of upbringing and education would you give it, what are the most important values you would share with a child, what about religion? Filling out the application is challenging, but it is an opportunity for Shogo and me to become very clear on what our values are. So we send in our application and wait.

Bloodlines

"Japan is a difficult country to adopt from," everyone says. Not only are there few children up for adoption, but it's the only country in the world where you need to get the extended family's approval for the process.

Bloodlines are seen as all-important, one's ancestors are one's link to the past. The family registry or *koseki* goes back generations and lists each birth and marriage, tying family to family. When we got married, I did not take my husband's name, and this caused a commotion at the ward office, as the clerk said there was no "official space" to put my own name on the form.

My husband stood his ground. "Well, *make* a space," he said, knowing that was impossible. One thing about bureaucracy is that it most definitely *cannot* make a space.

It would have been much easier for him to request or insist that I change my name, but he didn't. He just waited for the bureaucrat to find a way to remedy the situation. I kept my own name and was added to the *koseki*.

Then doubts start to flood my mind. If we succeed in adoption, I'll be bucking the system again.

I know how difficult it is to raise a child, let alone one who is adopted in a country that is not particularly "open" to adoption. In Japan, most adoptions are kept secret. Some children don't even find out until their parents die.

So we brace ourselves and ask my husband's father for permission. I find out, to my surprise, that his own father was adopted. Samurai on one side, gangster on the other. My husband has them all in his ancestry—geisha, gangster, samurai, rickshaw driver. This assortment of characters pleases me, makes me feel less strange for my difference, more welcome. My father-in-law says "yes."

We ask his sister, since she lives with us. She says "yes."

We breathe a big sigh of relief. But still I worry. All the possible scenarios tumble through my mind: I am a Westerner, and the child will not look like me, so everyone will know he or she is adopted. I know of foreign women who don't take their half-Japanese children to school as their children are ashamed and don't want their peers to know they are "*hafu.*" And because he is "different," I don't want him or her to be the victim of *ijime*, school bullying. That could lead to *hikikomori*, someone afraid to leave the house who spends his childhood at home. Even worse, it could lead to *jisatsu* or suicide. I know I am being neurotic, already thinking about the difficulties the child will face in grade school, middle school, junior high, high school and beyond. I know I am already being a mother.

I share my fears with my husband. He was beaten up in school, too.

"We turned out okay," he says. It was why I studied karate and meditation, which ultimately led me to Japan.

"Yeah, but we got our asses kicked a lot!"

"Maybe *we* went through it so our child wouldn't have to," he says.

"That's a nice thought," I shake my head. If only that's how it worked.

We decide that we are already a rainbow family, he with his long hair and stay-at-home job, me with my red streaks and funky yoga studio, not to mention our strange pit-bull mutt and his family's eccentric lineage. In a conservative neighborhood in a conservative country, we already stand out as freaks. Why not embrace it completely?

Perpetual Yes

In September, the agency calls about a little girl. We say "yes." Nothing happens. In December, they call about a boy. We wait. They offer the child to another family. Many young couples are waiting to adopt, and we are low on the list due to our ages.

I have to do something proactive. I am fiercely committed to living my dreams. If I'm not, who else will be? I contact a dozen international adoption agencies. Most of them don't write back. The few who do bother to respond say they don't work with families who live abroad. We apply in Vietnam. We wait some more.

Finally, I make Shogo call the orphanage. I insist that he tell them to stop calling us every month to ask if we are interested in a different child.

"Tell them to put a perpetual `yes' on our file, ok? Tell them that whatever child they have available, we are interested."

"Whatever child?"

"Yes. Whatever child."

I want to say all those things like "It isn't fair," and "Why us?" but I already know the answers to those questions, that there are no answers. This is our fate, our journey, our path.

And somehow, miraculously, it works.

The little boy they called us about a few months ago is available again.

"Yes!" we say, eager to meet the child who is destined to be ours.

But when they come to our house to tell us about him,

the information is sketchy at best.

"Do you have a picture?" I ask.

No picture.

This astounds me. More people have cameras in Japan than they have driver's licenses. Japan is the land of the camera—how could they not have a picture?

"Are you interested or not?" they ask. They're not messing around with this child. He's suffered enough.

"We're interested," we say together.

And for the second time in my life, I get down on my knees and pray.

Mothering Zen

Feb 1, 2007

We visit Yuto in the orphanage for hours, days, weeks, months. Finally, we can bring him home for an overnight. Then, finally, we can bring him home forever, just after his second birthday.

We go to a playground where he can see the bullet trains passing overhead. At the playground, he comes up to the other kids and wants to play with their toys, or play with their balls, or play with them in general. He likes to hold hands. He wants contact, touch, closeness. Because he grew up in an orphanage where everything was communal, he misses it. He has no concept of personal ownership.

The first time we give him Ai-Ai, the stuffed monkey we'd brought to take with him in the car—he tries to leave it behind at the orphanage. We have to convince him that he can keep it: he's never had a single thing of his own.

He is the opposite of other kids, who have to learn how to share. He brings his own toys to share, but the other kids don't take much interest in them. I don't want to try to make sense of things like this, or explain everything to him He'll learn. I want to cut a path in this crazy forest of life with him. Sitting Zen. Walking Zen. Playing Zen. Mothering Zen. It's all practice, and we have a lifetime.

But my aunt doesn't. I want him to meet her before she dies.

So we bring him to San Francisco. He loves his seven-year-old cousin Shaviv, but he cannot pronounce *Sh*, so he calls him Habib. My sister tells me Habib means "friend" in Hebrew.

We see a homeless man with a cat on the street in front of Macy's on Union Square. The cat has been hit by a car and the man needs money for its hospital bills. Everyone rushes by the man and the cat, but Yuto pulls my arm, insists on petting the cat. Then he sits down on the pavement and tries to pick up the cat to hug it. I tell him the cat is hurt and he shouldn't touch it. So he pets it instead. Now people stop to look at the little boy sitting on the sidewalk, blocking their way. Some mothers pull their children away. A photographer stops to take a picture. Others put money in the basket. More children come to sit by his side.

Somehow, he brings together the splintered worlds of strangers. He is a healer of cats and hearts, a small wonder in this world of so many wonders. If I ever felt any doubts, I do not now.

All That has Divided Us Will Merge

September 14, 2007

Though there are many customs for birth in Japan—the mother returning to her parents' house, a celebration of the child's first solid foods—we've missed them all. So we return to California to hold a Jewish baby naming ceremony for Yuto. Many people from my mother's community gather to welcome him, though we are strangers. Yuto is given the name Benjamin after his maternal grandfather, who came from Ludz, Poland, and Walter Benjamin, the Jewish writer/philosopher and member of the resistance in WWII. There is a ceremony where we throw all of our sins into the Napa River. Any time between Rosh Hashana and Yom Kippur, in the Jewish tradition, it is customary to throw breadcrumbs into a body of water as a symbolic act of repentance. The ritual is called Tashlich, A Sending Out. We gather at a waterfront to "cast away" the sins of the past and resolve to have a better year in the year to come.

My mother and stepfather, father and stepmother, my sisters and their sons are there. The whole family has gathered to heal and rejoice. All over the world, it is a holy time. In India it is the Ganesha festival, honoring the elephant god of new beginnings and remover of obstacles. In the Muslim world, it is Ramadan.

My mother's friends, most of whom I don't know, come up to congratulate us. Some tell me their stories, of how they too were adopted, or how they have adopted children, and what a wonderful *mitzvah* it is.

Tossing bread into the water, everything is still. It is a beautiful moment.

The congregation has prepared a special blessing for the occasion. It says:

May the one who blessed your ancestors bless you. We hope that you will be a blessing to everyone you know, humanity is blessed to have you.

Yuto sits atop his father's shoulders wearing his beaded yarmulke, smiling and dancing. Yuto is Jewish and Japanese, he is universal.

I look at Shogo and see that he is crying, too.

Humanity is blessed to have you.

The adults gather and say the Shabbat prayer:

And then all that has divided us will merge
Then compassion will be wedded to power
And then softness will come to a world that is harsh
    and unkind
And then both women and men will be gentle
And then both men and women will be strong
And then no person will be subject to another's will
And then all will be rich and free and varied
And then the greed of some will give way to the needs of
    many
Then all will share equally in the Earth's abundance
And then all will care for the sick and the weak and the old
And then all will nourish the young
And then all will cherish life's creatures

And then all will live in harmony with each other and
the environment
And then everywhere will be called Eden once again.

My mother has ordered a special cake for Yuto
decorated with a Pokemon character, though Yuto seems to
be the only one there who does not know what Pokemon is.
He devours the cake, which says: "Mazel Tov, Yuto. Welcome
to the Tribe."

April, 2008
My aunt passes away. I am stricken with grief. She is my
beloved, my friend, my mentor, my guide. But I cannot cry
forever. Yuto has been given a pogo stick and wants to
bounce on the sidewalk. It is dangerous, but he can't be
stopped. He seems impervious to pain, though I know he is
not. It's just that he learned not to cry at the orphanage,
where help might not have been as quick and as plentifully
as it might otherwise have come.

Suddenly, he points to the pavement.

"*Cho cho! Cho cho!*"

A butterfly lays on the ground. A beautiful orange and
black monarch.

"*Nette imasu,*"— it's sleeping. I use the Japanese euphe-
mism for death.

He leans over its lifeless body. "*Shinda?*" he asks. Is it
dead?

I wonder how, and where, he has learned that word.

"Yes," I say, scooping up the butterfly in my hands and
bringing it over to the garbage.

But this will not do.

"*Hana! Hana*," he stomps his feet and motions to a potted daisy bush in front of the house. Understanding, I carry the butterfly over and put it to rest on the bed of flowers. He covers it with a leaf. Then he points up. "*Sora*," he says. Sky.

Satisfied, he takes my hand and leads me back to the pogo stick, where he bounces and bounces until dinner time.

Carrying On
by Katherine Barrett

I leaned on the kitchen counter and studied the newspaper. Forty dead so far. Some knifed, some beaten, some burned alive. Scores more with torched houses and every last possession stolen, left homeless in the lashing winter rains. Why? Because they weren't born here. They are immigrants and refugees from bordering countries and a handful of violent South Africans have decided they must go home or die.

Jon tugged on the leg of my jeans. "I want pick up," he said, as he does a dozen times a day.

"Just a minute, sweetie..." I was on edge and wanted to finish the article. We had moved to South Africa from Canada only three months earlier, and my knowledge of this country's past and current struggles was sketchy and second-hand. I needed the newspapers to explain the brewing violence and convince me that it would stop. There are millions of foreign nationals in South Africa. I am one, but the vast majority are from troubled African countries. They have come here to find refuge and opportunity, but South Africa still struggles to house and employ its own. So now there is backlash....

"Mommy, I want pick UP!"

"Okay, love." I swung around to lift my two-year-old into my arms, to kiss his cheek and make sure his feet were warm. In that gesture, I was torn from the why, the what-if, the how-could of the world and planted firmly in the here-and-now of my children. It was a gesture known to all mothers, a gesture of carrying on despite politics and worry and irritation and self.

In the second between leaving the newspaper and reaching Jon, however, my mind flashed to another mother, probably not far from our home. I imagined her mirroring my actions, waiting anxiously for news that the violence had ended, hoping for assurance that her family would be safe. Small children tugged at her clothing, demanding her attention. Like mine, they were too young to grasp the events, just old enough to sense agitation in their mother. And she too, tore herself from the tensions of the world, to give her children another slice of bread or another hug.

We are foreigners in South Africa, myself and the woman in my mind. During the horrific violence in May 2008, we were linked by our thoughts of home, by an aching concern for our children, and by a resolution that, as mothers, we would carry on even as a national crisis stirred.

Despite our similarities, however, we are a universe apart. I have lived in South Africa a couple of months, moved here voluntarily as part of my husband's work and plan to return to Canada within a few years. The mother I imagined has lived here a decade perhaps, moved in desperate hope of a better life and planned never to leave. She is African and poor; I am Canadian and middle-class. Those differences carve out a chasm. They shape what we experience as daily struggles and how we are affected by extraordinary events such widespread xenophobic violence.

They mean, both now and in general, that she is less insulated, more vulnerable and that I, in all likelihood, will be fine.

Disparity and beauty. These were my first and lingering impressions of South Africa. We landed at the Cape Town airport last January, myself, my husband and our three young children. After piling suitcases into a rental car, we set out toward our new suburban home. Along the way, we greeted an infinite line of serrated, purple-hued mountains like visitors awed by their welcoming committee. We drove through foothills covered in ripening grapes and dotted with blue-gum trees. In the distance, we glimpsed the shine of the Atlantic. Above it all, an expressive and open sky.

At last we reached a neighborhood not unlike the one we left in North America: family homes with gardens and backyards and tidy driveways. It was familiar and would have been quite unremarkable were it not for the neighborhoods we passed to get here. For between the purple-hued mountains and the sparkling ocean, edging the wondrous sky and our comfortable suburban home, are townships and informal settlements—the legacy of apartheid.

While apartheid laws are gone and, I'm told, life for the poor is marginally better, inequality remains entrenched in South Africa. Homes in the townships, for instance, bear little resemblance to my own. Passing though, I see shacks of wood, concrete, corrugated iron and other salvaged materials. Some are constructed well enough to shade the summer heat and stall the winter rains; many are not. Some have running water, electricity, working sewers and garbage collection; many do not.

Disparity, like beauty, is not confined to South Africa. Even in Canada, there are inequalities of history and economics, of race and gender. No doubt I will see my home country differently when I return. But disparity in South Africa, to me at least, is shocking. It has forced me to recalibrate my scale of hardship and rethink what it means, as a mother, to carry on.

There have been times, during the past four years of parenting, when the thought of another endless, sleepless day-night-day was unbearable. I have three beautiful children, but bore them all within fifteen months. Pregnancy, birth and early infancy took a toll on my almost forty-year-old body and mind. The toddler and preschool years have brought more sleep but added the challenge of tantrums—at least two at a time—and running—in three divergent directions.

It would be easy to complain and I do. I'm as cranky as a tired toddler, in fact, when at five-thirty in the morning three demanding children crowd around my pillow and shout: "Mommy, wake up! Mommy, no sleeping!" and I must get out of bed, knowing that I will not have more than a moment to myself for the next fifteen hours. My patience wears after a morning of sibling bickering and complete disregard for maternal authority. And I snap, occasionally, when dwarfed by dirty laundry, ambushed by snack-seeking kids, and faced with an almost empty fridge. In other words, I complain about similar things as many middle-class, North American mothers of several children. I love my kids; I love being a mother. But at times I feel oppressed by a job that tolerates no days off and no off days.

On the verge of a mommy-meltdown, I might remind myself that I have, at least, a roof over my head and three meals a day. These are worn cliches—vacuous and trite—in the context of my Canadian motherhood, however. I take a sturdy roof and a decent meal, and a whole lot more, for granted. I have never questioned their existence. Nudge those cliches into a new reality however, transplant them into an entirely foreign culture, and their meaning returns with a jolt.

Suppose, for instance, that my children did not egg me out of bed at five-thirty but rather I rose voluntarily at four-thirty. I rose to do the laundry—outside, by hand—so the clothes could dry in the morning sun and the kids could wear their only warm sweaters by nightfall. Consider that three children under four years old is a small family, an easy load, when I might well have taken in several more children, claimed them as my own and struggled to feed them, simply because those children had nowhere else to go. Or imagine that I have lived as an immigrant in this country for many years, lived peacefully and productively but must suddenly shelter my children from the violent hatred of our neighbors.

Months have now passed since xenophobic violence erupted in South Africa. The anxious edge is blunted and the country is left with gaping questions, shame and thousands of homeless. Where is the other mother, the woman I imagined? Perhaps she has returned to her routines—much more worn, much more wary—sent her older children back to school and kept the younger ones by her side. She may have retreated to her home country, accepting uncertainty there over violence and alienation here. Or she could well be in limbo, camping in a temporary shelter, relying on goodwill for blankets, soap and food.

In comparison, my life was unmarred by the violence, but I am not unchanged. To me, the events last May were a grisly and graphic lesson in disparity—what it breeds and the myriad marks it leaves. Violence brought the struggles of this country, particularly those of women and mothers, into sharper focus. It has left me with greater appreciation as well as gnawing guilt for a relatively privileged life. It has roused a ferocious instinct to protect my children as well as a visceral urge to help others.

It is difficult to write about culture, especially an unfamiliar one, without stereotyping. South Africa is a convoluted country; there are a million stories and exceptions to every generality. I'm wary of painting contrasts too starkly, of erasing the richness of every life. I'm also wary of implying that North American mothers are a gaggle of pampered whiners. Mothering is hard—everywhere. But the sweeping differences between Canada and South Africa, even my most instant impressions, are enough to reposition myself on the scale of parental trials, and to instill profound respect for women who carry a load far greater than mine, and carry on despite hardship I can barely fathom.

Ghost Stories
by Stacy M. Lewis

We arrive at the beginning of winter. It's a synchronous ninety-nine degrees Fahrenheit and ninety-nine percent humidity. Rom carries our son in the backpack, and I lead our suitcases by their handles out of the luggage area. Rom's sisters Joy and Tata are there to greet us. Although everyone understands and speaks English—and speaks it because of me—there is still a lot I don't understand. Like where Rom's brother, Kiking, is. Like who the people are that have just approached us and reassured us that they recently saw Kiking and that he should be here in a few minutes. Rom tells me that they are "making business" and that they don't know Kiking, but everyone is polite enough to act as if they do.

Kiking doesn't show up, and as we start to go on our way, the other people offer to carry our luggage. Everyone knows they are making business, and everyone is polite enough to let them. We head across the street and upstairs to where we are supposed to meet Kiking (I think). There we meet up with Kiking's wife, Chona, and two of their three children, Albert and Inday. I think the little café where we sit down is still part of the airport. Five members of the wait-staff are lined up, ready to serve us our glasses of juice. We're the only customers.

Our two-year-old son, Orlando, was instantly at home

upon our arrival. He has never been to the Philippines before, but we stepped off the plane and soon he was laughing and running, playing with his cousins, perfectly content. He doesn't even seem hot.

We wait a long time for Kiking, but he doesn't show up. He may have had to take Mama back to the house to wait for our arrival. After drinking mango juices, we all traipse back downstairs and back across the street, carrying our own luggage this time—the business-makers must be somewhere else making business—to the place we started out. As far as I can gather, *this* is where we are supposed to meet Kiking. Eventually, he shows up in the mini-minivan we've rented during our stay, bringing with him Rom's other sister, En-en; his third child, Dudong; and Tata's two kids, Bernard and Farrah-Mae. We stow the luggage and pack ourselves into the car … seven adults and six kids.

Kiking shows his ID at the entry of the gated community where we're renting a house. The house is small, as most things in the Philippines are. It's clean and compact. Mama is in the back room, resting. Rom goes back first, and then I come in. She's sitting on the edge of the bed. Because she is sitting, I kneel down in front of her. I take her right hand in mine, the way a man of the court would take the hand of a lady, and then I hold her hand to my forehead. *Amin*, a sign of respect for my elders. She is so thin, and sick. This is why we came. To see Mama, and so our son could meet his *lola* (grandma). My son amins his lola, for the first and only time that trip.

He refuses, throughout the rest of our stay, to amin his lola. I remain steadfast in not forcing my son to do things, but my modeling and clear expectations are not holding up here. I am embarrassed at the indulgence of my American son, (a good Filipino child might shyly decline, would never run in the other direction with an unmistakable, quite culturally specific two-year-old "No!"), and I brim with grief at this one and last chance for him to know his grandmother. I watch, deflated, as my son squirms away.

It was my husband who insisted on staying in the subdivision. I told him we could stay with his family or somewhere closer, but he was emphatic: "No, we need somewhere nice this time." The last time we came, before our son was born, we had an apartment a short tricycle-taxi ride away from his childhood home. The apartment was leaky and full of cockroaches. Many houses here are not sealed off from the outside; the doors don't quite reach the ground; there are no screen windows, sometimes no windows, just slats that can be opened or closed based on the sun's slant or the rain's angle. The apartment wasn't furnished. I found out later that his family had brought the furniture from their own house before our arrival and that they'd been living in further reduced circumstances during our stay. We bought a futon, a toaster oven, and many other things, all of which we left with them when we returned to the States.

Rom and I met at work, in Seattle. He uncharacteristically and promptly asked me on a date and I tried to hold out—we *were* working together—but he was too dang cute, and we couldn't stop talking to each other, sharing the long stories of our lives. He told me about his family—his brother and sisters and mom who all still lived in the Philippines. He told me about his father, who was a lawyer. He had died of cancer ten years earlier, and it was becoming clear that the family was losing its tenuous foothold on middle-class life. They all lived in the house where Rom grew up, though Kiking had moved his wife and three kids into the now defunct little store that had been built in front of their house, right up against the sidewalk-less street, a five-by-eight-foot cement-block building, a vestige of one of his mother's endeavors to "make business."

After we were married, family members often called us, asking for help with this or that bill, or this or that project, or tuition to go back to school to get a better-paying job. They faced a continual struggle to get ahead, which often resulted—because their money got tied-up in *utang* (debt)—in them staying exactly where they were, or worse, falling further behind.

Rom also told me about the island in the Philippines where he grew up. I told him about the island in Alaska where I grew up. His island's name was tongue-foreign to me. I had no idea what letters it took to spell Cebu (pronounced seh-boo). He told me that the places he had played as a kid—the river, the fields, the fishing ponds— were gone, the land pockmarked by developments of all kinds. A box-making shop here, open-fire roadside eateries everywhere, a slaughterhouse and canning operation there, and shell-making and wood-working companies to appease the tourist trade. The unregulated small and medium-sized businesses and a lack of infrastructure create devastating pollution. People keep coming from the rural areas into the city to find opportunity, and they live in unbelievably small makeshift houses, some on stilts above the river, which is now clogged with garbage, human waste, and clothing. The river, which is now a strip of saddened and freighted sludge, carries the cost of humans and their opportunities to the open sea, where it dissipates and becomes dilute. Though even in the open sea, the coral is mostly dead, dynamited by people hoping to catch the greatest amount of fish in the cheapest and fastest way possible.

Rom's earliest memory is waking up in the morning and seeing the sun rising out the open window. Rom is the first-born son, and as such, his father decided it was his destiny to become a lawyer. Like father, like son. As a teenager, Rom used to lie on the roof of his house, watching the airplanes fly above him. He knew someday he would fly on one to America. In his last year of law school at a prestigious Philippine university, he applied to the Art Center School of Design in Pasadena. He was accepted and won a Philippines-wide Rotary Scholarship for one year's tuition and travel expenses. He eventually told his mother what he was doing. She and his older sister tried to persuade him against it, but, in the end, his mom helped him and kept it a secret from his father.

When his dad found out, he left the family in a silent rage. He returned to his home island and sent his relatives, one by one, to tell Mama that his dreams had been dashed and that Rom needed to stay in law school. Eventually his dad came back. For a while they all pretended that Rom would be going back to law school. And then, after Rom left for the States, his father, to save face—and to shield his broken heart—began to live the lie that his son was going to

America to become a lawyer. He flew with Rom as far as Manila, and then said goodbye to his first-born son.

After Rom's first airplane flight, in which he flew across the world and landed in summertime Los Angeles, where he was freezing, he called his mom. They cried together on the phone. Rom told me that he knew right then that nothing would be the same for him, ever again. My future husband had dislocated himself from his family and his home country. When I look at our son, Orlando, I try to imagine how his father's dislocation will eventually re-locate itself in him.

Rom's demeanor changes the moment we land in the Philippines. He seems taller, more settled, capable, and sort of excited. There's a smile behind his eyes. At the same time, he can seem terribly sad, and he talks often about how things used to be. He is home, truly and overwhelmingly so, yet he spends most of our time there antsy to return to Seattle.

I am simply here, in the Philippines, accompanying my husband. Staying at the subdivision house reinforces my sense of remove and heightens my sense of being the spoiled American. Rom tells me that Filipinos "love" Americans (spoiled or not), but I feel remote and ogled. People stare. People see me walking down the street, and they keep their gaze steady, unbelieving, and watch Rom and me go by. My first visit, I would see them looking, and upon making eye contact, I would smile. Nobody smiled back. Since it's not considered rude to stare, there is no need to offset the tension (or aggression) with a smile. They just keep staring, as much at me—light reddish hair, pale freckly face, not tall in the States but taller than most here—as they are at the spectacle of a *balikbayan* (returning native Filipino) with an American woman.

The little kids, excited, point and yell "Americana!" then cover their mouths and run away. Or they say in English, "Ma'am, ma'am, what's your name?" When I respond with the little Cebuano I know, they nearly fall over and then run away.

Rom tells me that everyone in the Philippines "loves" *mestiso* (mixed) children, too. Tata tells Rom that Orlando is "so cute, like the Gerber baby." Everyone in my family thinks that Orlando looks like Rom; everyone in Rom's family thinks Orlando looks like me. When I was pregnant, my mom would tease us, "You each want the baby to look like the other one." The Other. I imagined the baby inside me, in that murky, smoky way you do, and she was right: I saw a little brown baby with dark, wavy hair, brown eyes. Our baby, in my mind's eye, always had Rom's eyes.

What did Rom see? A little pale baby, with reddish hair, freckles, and apparently, not green (like mine) but *blue* eyes.

Eye color inheritance turns out to be a lot more complex than those Mendelian peas I learned about in high school biology, but the scientific literature makes it pretty clear that one brown-eyed person with a long history of brown eyes and one green-eyed person will almost certainly make a brown-eyed baby. But Rom kept holding out.

"Honey," I would say, "but only if you have any blue- or green-eyed ancestors. Do you think you do?" He would seem proud that it wasn't likely (meaning that his family has remained more or less indigenous) yet dreamy about the possibility. He would flash a flirty smile, *"Diba."* (Could be.)

When Orlando was born, he was pale-ish, had dark, straight hair (with streaks of red-gold in it). He had one freckle (on his forearm), his father's flat nose, and brown eyes, brown like the deepest, richest moss. And Rom, after reading that it can take time for eye color to settle (usually from light to dark, but no matter), asked, "Do you think maybe his eyes will turn blue?"

I opened my eyes wide so he could seem them clearly and said, "*My* eyes aren't even blue!"

"But," he says, "what about Mercedes?" Mercedes is from Puerto Rico. She told us how her dad wanted her to look like him and when she was born, she did: dark curls, olive skin, brown eyes. And then, right before his very eyes, she faded into her mother's coloring … her hair straightened and turned blond, her skin sprouted freckles, and then, gasp! *Her brown eyes turned blue on her second birthday.*

My husband holds onto the anecdotal, the unusual, the supernatural, the miraculous. I laugh, realizing how nice it is, thinking of our child as holding within him all possibilities. To think that maybe if we're lucky enough, or look closely enough, we will see magic happening before our very own eyes.

"How do you say green in Cebuano?"

Rom is silent for a moment, his eyes turned upward, searching his brain for the word, "I can't remember." He gives an embarrassed, almost triumphant laugh.

When our son, Orlando, was a tiny baby, Rom spoke mostly in Cebuano to him, but as time went on, he spoke it less and less. Now Rom speaks to him almost exclusively in English.

Rom says he "can't really remember it all," or that he's "more comfortable in English." There is no one in Rom's life to speak Cebuano with, except his family, via phone. And even then, the language is full of English (and Spanish) words. Some were incorporated into the language long ago; some are short-hand for the becoming-forgotten Cebuano words, either individually or culturally. The words are English or Spanish; the pronunciation is not.

We have a joke now. I ask Rom, "How do you say green in Cebuano?"

He answers quickly, imbuing the word with the clipped Cebuano cadence, "Glin."

Rom and I often ask ourselves if we should try to find some Filipinos here in Seattle so Rom can converse in Cebuano, and Orlando can hear and participate. Rom tells me, most of the Filipinos in the States are from up north. At first I am not sure why this matters, but being made up of more than seven thousand islands, the Philippines is a fractious nation, replete with many different cuisines, customs, dialects. What Rom would end up having in common with these Filipinos is, ironically enough, English.

Apparently, traveling all the way to the Philippines and surrounding ourselves with family won't teach my son the Cebuano language, either. Everyone is too polite to keep speaking Cebuano, so they speak English. Orlando could care less what language they speak. He runs off with his cousins without a second glance at us.

Rom arrived in the States at the age of twenty-four. He has told me, many times, that he was never alone until he came to this country. I believe him. His house was well-populated—by his mother, his father, his maternal grandmother, and distant relatives from his father's island and his mother's home village whom Rom refers to as the "maids," women who came to the city to make money by taking care of the kids. When I first heard Rom say the word maids, I remember thinking, Who is this guy? Was his family rich? They had *maids*?

I now know a little bit more about how "rich" works in the Philippines. Rich means if you have money, any amount of money, you hire all the people you can to spread the wealth around. Even the stores there employ an abundance of help, with three people at the checkout stand: one to ring up your purchase; one to wrap it precisely in scratchy yellow paper and put it into a plastic bag with ties at the top; one to staple your receipt to the outside of the bag and hand you your completed purchase. And someone else to say good-day to you as you exit the store.

The streets there display a continual parade of humanity—the small homes crowd the road, and people sit on their porches, combing their hair, tending their cooking fires, hanging their clothes to dry. They walk the dirt strips between asphalt and scrubby grassed areas where goats are tied and chickens peck. Cars drive the roads amid a sea of silver and brightly-colored jeepneys, diesel-spewing tricycle taxis, and ploddingly determined pedicabs, fueled by the energy of a hungry person. The jeepneys (American Army jeeps left over from World War II that have been transformed into privatized buses) carry dozens of people inside, their faces framed by the cut-out, glass-less windows, and a dozen more outside, their bodies balanced on the bumper, their hands holding on where they can. The tricycles themselves carry close to a dozen people. (Imagine a motorcycle with a sidecar: In the sidecar there are four adults, sitting on seats the size of bricks; on the back of the bike, behind the driver, there are two adults, maybe a kid or two, or three.) The pedi-cabs carry their modest loads soberly, persistently, down the road, fading into the dark.

In America, I spend my days alone with my toddler son, endeavoring to make connections with other people—my neighbors, the parents at the park, someone, anyone. I talk to my mother long-distance on the telephone. In America, Rom and I walk in our neighborhood with our son and listen to the sounds of no one home. The homes in the Philippines are physically porous, and the people, too, spill through the cracks, and live their lives just as much around their homes as in them. Rom and I ask ourselves here in the heart of our "family-friendly" neighborhood, *Where could all the people be?* We sometimes hear the shouts of children or smell barbecue smoke coming from back yards, but mostly we see closed-up homes, hollow porches, no one making a little business on the sidewalk, no one walking to or from home at the end of the day. Rom and I ask ourselves, *Where are our people?*

One of the first stories Rom told me was about the haunted house his family lived in for a short time when he was young. It took his father longer to realize the ghosts' presence than his mother. One night, finally having had enough of sick children, mysterious noises, and gray-haired old ladies appearing on their front porch, he said to the spirits of the place, "Come out and show yourselves!" He was, the story goes, swept off his feet and thrown down the stairs. They moved out soon after.

On our first visit to the Philippines, Rom casually mentioned the tree spirits to me, raising his eyes and hand lazily up to the green canopy that spread over the front of their house.

"The what?" I asked him.

Rom grew up with stories from his mother about the *engkanto* (fairies who live in trees, to whom you should always be polite, saying hello and letting them know you're just passing by) and the *agta*, a seven-foot, cigar-smoking dark giant who also lives in trees and likes to court young women. Mama likes to tell stories, stories about ghosts, spirits, sprites, the life force.

On this trip, I ask Rom again about the tree spirits. Orlando, who is on Rom's lap and who is usually trying to keep me and my husband from talking to each other, becomes still and quiet. He is the picture of the enthralled child—upturned face, his eyes wide, his mind utterly open and enchanted. He listens to Rom retell the stories from his own childhood … the *duwende* (dwarves who live in mushrooms), the *agta*, the *engkanto*, the *santilmo* (a person's life force that appears as a ball of fire), the *ungo* (vampires). Orlando asks him to repeat the stories, over and over. Although I'm the one who asked for these stories, my husband is no longer telling them to me. He's telling them to my son, who turns to me and exclaims, "You pour salt on the ungo's legs and it melts!"

I feel so pleased to see my son listening to his father's

stories, his lola's ghost stories, these specifically Filipino stories. The Philippine idea of a romanticized America creeps me out, but mustn't I admit that a very American smiley-faced attitude toward multiculturalism is the reason I feel so pleased? That I am romanticizing my own son's heritage? At the same time, I think, what exactly are these stories giving him, besides suspense and entertainment? But if these stories aren't good enough to be part of his heritage, what do I think is? His brown eyes? His Papa's pathological politeness? The politics of the Philippines and the world economy? An English sprinkled with Cebuano-inflected words? Who am I to monitor the ethnic content of these interactions between father and son?

We take Mama to the hospital for her radiation treatment. I learn that Mama thinks she is going to beat this thing, but that Rom and Joy know that the treatment, at this point, is purely palliative, to keep the tumor in her neck from growing and causing her too much discomfort. I think, in America we have the luxury of saying of a fatal disease, "I am going to beat this thing" and actually have a chance of doing so (if we have the money and the connections).

Mama could have come to the United States for treatment when her cancer was first discovered. Rom's sister Joy is a nuclear medicine doctor who treats cancer patients at a well-respected hospital in California, for Christ's sake. But Mama didn't want to come. She said she was afraid to travel alone. She said she wanted Tata to come with her (an impossible request, since Tata could never have gotten a visa). She didn't say, *I don't want to die in America.*

So Mama was treated in the Philippines—and she had better-than-most care there because of Joy's influence and because of her American children's money, but they botched her tracheotomy, and a year later, when we are here to visit, she still has the tube in her throat, which makes it difficult for her to talk, breathe and eat. She is so thin. She comes down with pneumonia (for the third time), and we stop the daily drives to the hospital because her radiation treatments have been postponed until she can regain her strength.

When it's time to leave the Philippines, Mama comes with us to the airport (everyone goes with everyone everywhere, but Mama had been staying home more). We have to pass through security to get to the gates, so we say our good-byes in a small corner where Mama has sat down to rest. Rom hugs his mom and tells her, "Don't lose hope." I am already crying, grasp Mama's hands and say, inexplicably, "Thank you." I keep crying.

She died three weeks later. She collapsed in the kitchen. Tata and Kiking couldn't tell if she had a pulse, but they called an ambulance right away. They waited for the ambulance that never came, and then put Mama in the car and drove her to the hospital themselves. She was revived upon arrival, and that's when they called us. Rom told me the story, and I said, "What's going to happen?"

"Kiking thinks there will be a miracle."

My husband spent the next two days with his eyes barely open. They were swollen not with tears (though there are those, too) but with an involuntary announcement: I need privacy for now. Which I tried to give him.

He and his siblings decided to move Mama to a private

room with a phone, and they decided that they would take her off life support. Rom talked to her on the phone for a long time in the middle of the night (she couldn't talk, but he knows she heard him). When I woke in the morning, he told me, "I talked to Mama. I said goodbye." His eyes were open.

We didn't try to hide from Orlando that we were sad or concerned or that something was happening to Mama. He heard us talking about Mama, then about her funeral, and he saw us crying. He wanted a red ribbon to wear, too, after Rom and I put on ours. Tata had told us that Mama's body was sweating, which meant she was having a hard time leaving this world. We wore red to let her know that it was okay for her to move on, that she needn't worry. Orlando didn't ask questions, and we didn't endeavor to explain it all to him. We'll tell him someday. Right now, his lola is still alive to him, just as his cousins are. They are members of his imaginary magical troupe of friends, family, and characters, to be called upon at will. To him, they don't live in any particular place or time; they simply live.

Before our evening meal, we acknowledge our connection to the food we are about to eat, and we share our hopes for our loved ones. We often say, "And our thoughts are with our family in the Philippines." After our visit, Orlando would take this as an opportunity to call out the names of his cousins, his aunts, his uncles, and his lola. It happens again tonight, and Rom and I repeat after him, "And, yes, Lola."

My son does not yet comprehend the miles that separate countries or the distances that live within families. He doesn't think of his Papa's ghost stories as specifically

Filipino. He doesn't recognize the politics and persistence of poverty or the historical veneer of colonialism. He doesn't fall prey to globalization's allure nor grimace in the face of its devastation. He isn't a witness to these things. Not yet.

We don't tell him that his lola is no longer in the Philippines, that perhaps she is in a magical place some call heaven, and we don't tell him the story about the differences between these two places. Not yet.

Fade to Brown

by Anjali Enjeti-Sydow

My favorite color is brown.

I know what you're saying. Brown? Really? Not blue or purple or even a sunshiny yellow?

Nope. It's brown. I love a deep, dark mocha. The color of slightly milky Darjeeling tea, the shade of walnut oak, the rich texture of a Hershey's milk chocolate bar. I favor, hands down, a sip from steaming hot cocoa to apple cider. I love the colors of autumn—the yellows and oranges and penetrating reds—but I prefer the hue of the crinkly, dry brown leaves long after they've expired from their branches.

Despite our one-quarter European heritage (we are also one-quarter Puerto Rican and half Indian), my brother and I both came out decidedly dark. We are both brown as brown can be. In the summer, we are even browner—a trip to the mailbox and back might color us a shade or two darker. There are no genetic hints of our pure Austrian grandmother who still pronounces "th" like a "d" due to her overwhelmingly thick German accent. Depending on the setting, most people assume we are one-hundred percent Indian. (Though some retail store owners in small towns watch us suspiciously as we finger their merchandise, concluding that we must be shoplifting Hispanics.)

When I look at myself in the mirror, I take great pride in the brown image before me. I have always loved being brown, despite the occasional insults it attracts. In youth, I was asked more than once, "Are you brown because your dad shit on you?" (Of my parents, my father is the brown one. Amazingly, bullies correctly guessed which parent to attribute said defecation to.) And then there was the ever so popular, "Why don't you just go back to your tribe?" Or its more cutting variation, "Are you going to scalp me?" (To which I was forced to explain that my father was from India. He never lived in a tee-pee or wore feathers or exposed the skulls of his enemies.) And because of my color, I have been called the N-word by children too young to understand its jarring significance.

Though their comments and actions were less obvious, when I grew older, people still had issues with my brownness. I never got parts in plays for characters that were traditionally white. When kids started "going together," my friends kept suggesting that I go with the other Indian or Asian or African American boy in the class, not the adorable, white Scandinavian. Parents acted justified in their spoken discrimination, as if their hipness to multiculturalism exempted them from the invidiousness of racism. Adults often proclaimed in a complimentary yet condescending tone that I spoke flawless English (the only language I've ever known), and asked whether I've ever eaten typically American dishes such as meat loaf. My senior calculus teacher seemed surprised if I ever got a B on an exam—the other Asian brown kids scored in the high 90s without opening a book.

My brownness has even projected political turmoil. At the height of Desert Storm, I prematurely fled the Wendy's counter before picking up my baked potato and side of chili, because the men behind me were casting such evil eyes at my back while angrily cursing about "those fucking A-Rabs." As soon as I reached the door to the restaurant, they bust out laughing while yelling, "Where do you think you're going, Darkie?" I was shaking so badly by the time I got to the car, I could hardly get the key in the ignition. And then there was the delight of travel post-9/11. On one particular trip, I was flagged as a security risk on each leg of the flight, not to mention, at the ticket counter itself. No matter. I had highly entertaining conversations with all the other brown, now shoeless people who had also been pulled to the side. And on two other trips, my oldest daughter, who at the time was still in size three diapers, took her turn at being felt up by a magnetized prod. Even though she was just a brown, drooling infant, she was still required to do her part to combat The War on Terror.

None of it, though—the harassment, the mean stares, or the singling out—none of it has ever made me wish I were white. I still love me brown.

I married a man who is half Hispanic. He is significantly lighter than me, but still possesses a healthy olive glow to his skin and tans well during the summer. In other words, I did not see him as a threat for the genetic erasure of brown skin in my children. I thought our offspring might be lighter, but I knew they'd be at least a little brown. I secretly reveled in the fact that they would probably never "pass" for white.

Mira, who was born six years ago, came out just as brown as I am. It was plain to see that in the making of our lovely daughter, there was no dance of light and dark chromosomes. Mira's flesh absorbed all of my mocha. There was no dilution of brownness whatsoever.

Two years later, my second daughter, Leela, was born. Oh, she was just as beautiful in every way—the perfect embodiment of ten fingers and ten toes.

Except that she was white.

At first, I didn't lose hope. Some babies are born lighter, and then steadily darken as they get older. Perhaps Leela's tanness was dormant and would appear fashionably late.

But a brown tone did not metamorphose. Leela was and is white. There is a slight peachy undertone to her form and her cheeks are a lovely rose when she plays outside in the heat. But there is no shadow, no tan, no darkness, no brown. If I were to outfit Leela in a Lederhosen and ship her off to her Austrian relatives who still reside in Linz, she'd fit right in. Every sign of brown ethnicity—Indian and Hispanic— has eluded her. She is even fairer than my half-Hispanic husband.

I'll be honest here. Leela's skin color has caused me some distress. Not because I don't think she'll look good in pastel colors, or because I now have to be extra careful about sunscreen, or because she'll likely have to wear foundation to avoid looking pale. I fear that Leela won't empathize with her brown sister's life experiences in a society that still favors the fair. Or worse, that Leela will simply ignore what Mira will inevitably undergo. That she'll attribute any injustice that Mira experiences to a host of other factors, but never, particularly in situations when it's otherwise obvious, to her color. I worry that because Leela is white, Mira, in this world where beauty is defined by whiteness, will not think that she's as pretty. Or worse, that she will not feel as valued. That while Mira will have to avoid playing near the tire swing because of the rotten kid who told her to go back to her own country, Leela will continue to romp around as she pleases, without noticing her sister's pained face. And I worry that Leela will have a luxury that her sister will never have—of recognizing only the most obvious manifestations of racism, while ignoring its toxic subtleties.

I'm afraid too, that Leela won't feel as connected to her brown ethnic background because she doesn't look the part. That she'll be excluded by Indians and Hispanics as a wannabe. That she'll feel silly wearing Indian bangles or *salwar kameez* on her white skin. I worry that Leela won't feel justified in her desire to take Bollywood dancing lessons or celebrate Diwali celebrations. That in a conversation with another Hispanic she won't reveal her shared Latino heritage and her love for Spanish rice and beans. I worry that she'll be perceived as some sort of multicultural poser. An ethnic fake. An individual who can avail herself of the vibrant cultural traditions of her brownness, but then escape its inherent discrimination. And if Leela benefits from all of the good of her background, and none of the bad, will Mira resent her? Will Mira envy her white sister's ability to go largely unnoticed in this country because she's the status quo?

By most of all, I fear that unlike me, Mira won't have a brown sibling to confide in when she faces the hatred of others. I worry that, because of this, she will feel isolated and alone. I worry that Leela won't be able to come up with the quick comeback to a racist taunt, the way my brother did for me. After all, my brother was my partner in brownness. My ally in ethnicity. My first line of defense in discrimination. He was my system of support against racism. I worry that Mira won't have this in her own sibling.

Perhaps my fears about the girls' difference in color are exaggerated. Perhaps I'm too sensitive, too suspicious of the actions of others. Perhaps I play the race card. I don't know. I still maintain the hope that the world is a better place. That the perception of a person is not a consequence of his or her color. But there is already talk about a racist teacher at the local elementary school, and my careful eavesdropping of conversations in school hallways, at birthday parties, and on playgrounds belie my optimistic beliefs. In a few years time, maybe less, the girls will know that their respective skin colors matter, and in very different ways.

Nevertheless, my wishes for my daughters are the same. I want them to grow up to be sensitive to other people. I want them to be advocates for others. I want them to speak out against injustice. I want them to acknowledge when either they or others face discrimination. But above all else, I want them to be sisters who stick by each other despite the fact that their differences in color will likely afford them diverse life experiences.

And I want them to love the colors of the skin they were born in, just as much as I do.

Mothering Across Cultures
by Angela Turzynski-Azimi

"But we're not in Australia, and we're not in Iran, and we're not in England—we're in Japan!" Six-year-old Kye is at the stage of beginning to challenge our adult reasoning, exposing its sometimes glaring illogicality. In this case, the issue concerned is the custom in Japan of allowing, or rather requiring, primary school-age children to walk to and from school unaccompanied by a parent or other responsible adult, a dilemma that we have not yet been able to resolve. Our patient explanations of how in Australia, Iran and England children do not walk alone to school have little meaning for Kye in his everyday world.

Kye was born in Australia, the adopted home of his parents, where he lived until the age of three. His mother was born and raised in the U.K., of English and Polish parentage. His father was born and raised in Iran. By some quirk of fate the paths of his British mum and Iranian dad crossed in Japan, where we became better acquainted through our common non-native language of Japanese, and from where we eventually went to Australia, married, and had Kye. Three years later, we returned to Japan as an Australian family, to introduce Kye to the country that had brought his parents together, and the culture that after a combined total of seventeen years had become an integral part of our own identities. Today, Kye has spent most of his life in Japan.

In navigating these cultural boundaries, language plays a significant and complex role, fascinating and challenging by turns. I remember back in the early days when Kye was just a few months old being taken aback by a comment made by a child health professional in Australia at a routine check-up. On learning that Kye's grandmother would soon visit us from Iran, and that she spoke only Persian, the nurse asked, "But how will she communicate with the baby if she doesn't speak English?" Leaving aside the fact that Kye's father had spoken Persian to him since the day he was born, it was quite a revelation to me to realize that the idea of someone communicating with a baby in a "foreign" language could be such an alien concept. Much later, I read about the way babies initially produce a diverse range of sounds, some of which are recognized as belonging to the language of their community and as such encouraged, and others simply ignored or met with unfavorable responses. According to this theory, babies quickly learn to stick with the sounds that earn them the positive reaffirmation of those on whom they depend for their well-being and ultimate survival. This articulated what I myself had sensed but what the nurse's comment had prompted me to realize was not necessarily the common perception.

In my own case, as was fairly typical in the north of England in the 1960s, I was not taught the language of my foreign-born father, whose main concern was that I and my siblings should blend in with the mainstream culture of my mother. While this worked well enough inside the immediate family unit, I felt a sense of dissatisfaction at extended family gatherings where I was unable to exchange more than the most basic greetings with my Polish grandparents, who spoke little English, and where I could not understand my aunts and uncles when they conversed in their native Polish.

Over time, it became apparent that I had a facility with foreign languages, an ability to memorize and reproduce unfamiliar sounds with relative ease, and I went on to learn other European languages before encountering Japanese. Such a focus on languages almost to the exclusion of other areas of study throughout my school years and beyond into my adult life only served to fuel what I would term a sense of loss in respect to the language of my father. This was further compounded by the loss I felt when he passed away just weeks before my son was born, and the realization that I would now never connect with my father through his own language made me even more determined that my son should not be deprived of his paternal linguistic heritage. If I wanted to understand what was being said between father and son, I believed that it was up to me to learn their language. Ironically, my command of Persian has never developed beyond a few words of greeting and basic vocabulary. Yet I do not feel shut out in any way. Rather, I enjoy listening to the sounds and rhythms of the language they share, and feel a sense of satisfaction that they have this special bond. At the same time, the switching and mixing of languages—Japanese, Persian, English—is something that we as a family choose not simply to tolerate but to celebrate, as a gift that offers us a unique form and breadth of expression and enriches our lives.

While Kye's facility with the Persian language is limited compared with that of his English mother tongue or his Japanese "daytime" language of communication, he displays a strong affinity with his father's culture. Last year, he was taken to visit Iran for the first time, to expose him to an environment where Persian is the majority language. As he is the child of an Iranian father, this meant we had to choose a new given name acceptable to the Islamic authorities for his identification papers. So for ten days, Kye became Kiarosh, and attended an Iranian kindergarten near his grandmother's home. I stayed behind in Japan, for a number of reasons. I felt that by doing so Kye would be able to fully experience his father's culture through his father's language, without relying on me for English back-up. I also knew, having visited Iran with my husband before we were married, that I would find it impossible to sit calmly in a car with my son unrestrained by a seat-belt in the crazy traffic of Tehran, yet I knew that this would be a daily reality. What is more, the issue of circumcision was bound to be a hot topic around the dining table given that Kye was five years old at the time. I have left the decision on whether, when, and where to do this up to my husband and, while I knew that he did not intend to have this carried out during that first visit to Iran out of a desire to give Kye a wholly positive experience, nevertheless I was aware that pressure might well be applied by my in-laws and I did not feel equipped to handle this kind of situation. Aside from these concerns, there was the very practical issue of my obtaining permission to enter Iran, which does not recognize our non-Islamic marriage, requiring a lengthy and troublesome visa application process. So I waved the two of them off at Japan's Narita airport, in their matching blue baseball caps, full of excitement and anticipation on my son's behalf.

Since that trip, Kye has spent a month in Australia, where he attended a pre-school and became re-acquainted with his home country. Yet today he insists that the place he wants to go and live one day is Iran. As if to drive this point home, he has replaced the Japanese *katakana* chart on the wall with the Persian alphabet chart, and goes through stages of faithfully copying out his Persian letters, which he then takes to school to share with his Japanese teachers and friends. I am thankful that we opted to educate Kye through the Montessori system, where this is respected as a valuable part of his mixed cultural identity. I must confess, however, that even I was surprised when he came home one day with a beautifully hand-made book containing only the first letter of the Persian alphabet carefully written out one hundred times!

When we lived in Australia, where there is a sizeable Iranian community, we would often go to local Iranian restaurants and grocery stores, to eat kebabs, buy Iranian-style bread, and enjoy a range of fresh dates, yoghurt, and iced desserts, as well as other traditional foods. We would also celebrate Persian New Year, or Nooruz, which falls on March twenty-first, the first day of spring in the northern hemisphere. In our family, we made this time a triple celebration, to mark my birthday and our wedding anniversary during the preceding two days. The Nooruz celebrations begin with the festival of Chahar Shambe Suri, a symbolic ritual held outdoors where families leap over small bonfires. Surrounded by the majestically tall and slender forms of Australia's indigenous eucalyptus trees, with the sound of traditional Iranian festival music blaring out in the background, Kye was duly carried over the flames in the arms of his father, then placed on the shoulders of his grown-up cousin to watch from the sidelines, entranced by the flickering flames illuminating the faces of the crowds.

Sometimes, we would have Kye's grandmother and other relatives visiting us from Iran during this period, which brought the Nooruz celebrations into the home. This included the Haftseen table, a ceremonial display of items symbolizing spring rebirth, joy, prosperity, and other such themes. As I write this I am reminded of how much Kye enjoyed this simple ritual, thrilled by the goldfish, representing life and the end of the zodiac sign of Pisces, and eagerly repeating the names of each of the objects after his aunty. And how, since coming to Japan, where we have no contact with other Iranians, we have made little effort to continue such traditions. I am led to wonder why, when we continue to observe a version of the Christmas rituals that I grew up with, including the Polish custom of celebrating with a family dinner on Christmas eve, we are becoming remiss about observing such important Iranian traditions? I believe that this in itself has its roots in culture, in that firstly, it is largely the women of the house who are responsible for the practical arrangements surrounding the Nooruz celebrations, so my husband feels less inclined to act as the initiator. And secondly, perhaps more importantly, the Nooruz celebrations cannot really exist without an extended network of family and friends from the same cultural tradition. The need for a wider Iranian community to celebrate at this time was brought home to me this year, when we received an invitation from the Iranian embassy in Tokyo to attend a Nooruz function. While some of the guests may already have been friends or acquaintances, I got the impression that there were many who were coming together simply to join other Iranians for the countdown to the New Year. As far as my own traditions are concerned, the Christmas rituals are not dependent on this wider network. So, although we are living in Japan where Christmas for most people is a commercially-driven event, the lack of a wider Western community does not prevent me from exposing Kye to some of the related traditions I grew up with. In fact, in some ways I feel that this is an advantage: having left Australia, where Christmas is a mainstream celebration, I can filter out the aspects of the Christmas culture with which I feel less comfortable, such as the materialistic pressures. Similarly, when it comes to birthday celebrations, I feel free to celebrate Kye's special day with as little or as much fuss as we choose, since birthday parties and gift or card-giving are not common here in Japan and so there are no expectations, whether on the part of friends or on the part of Kye himself.

The challenges we face lie elsewhere, such as the issue of Kye's walking unaccompanied to school. During my years of living in Japan as a single person I often observed young children carrying schoolbags traveling alone, either on foot or on public transport. Some were tiny, almost dwarfed by their backpacks. Like many people, I suspect, I interpreted this at face value as yet another indication of how safe Japanese society is. However, in my son's later pre-school years, as I spoke with the mothers of older children who were getting ready to start primary school, I became aware that the issue was somewhat complex. The mothers were clearly worried about letting their children walk alone. At that time it was not unusual to hear in the news of children, often girls, being abducted as they traveled to and from school. Some appeased their worry by having their children carry mobile phones, to enable them to call home if they were in trouble, or GPS satellite devices so that they could track their movements. Others settled for the safety alarm that is thrown in free with some schoolbags. One mother even told me how she had tried to persuade her daughter to choose a black schoolbag over a red one. While these days a multitude of colors is available, traditionally black is for boys and red is for girls. She reasoned that since her daughter was tall, sturdily built, and wore her hair short, she could be mistaken for a boy from a distance and as such would be a less likely target if she carried a black bag. The mother's efforts to persuade her were to no avail, and the girl insisted on the traditional red bag.

Gradually, I became a little more attuned to the issue. However, as I began to assemble the articles of clothing and other school supplies that my son would need to enter this new phase of his education, I was still far from understanding the significance of traveling unaccompanied to school as a mark of transition from pre-school child to primary school child. While some mothers may voice their concerns about this, it would appear to be unacceptable social practice to translate this into action. This is borne out by my conversations with mothers from Western countries, as well as Japanese mothers who have lived with their school-age children in Western countries, who have told me how the teachers at their children's Japanese schools reprimand them for accompanying their children and ask them not to do it.

Yet I was still not prepared for what I heard at the first meeting of the small group of parents of the children who would join my son in a class of six- to eight-year- old children at a new primary school. This was the first stage of expansion of the existing pre-school program, and as such the primary classroom would be in the same building as the pre-school. At this meeting, mothers who would be driving their younger children to the pre-school talked of how they planned to deliberately arrange their schedules so that they did not take the elder sibling—still perhaps only six years old—in the car. Similarly, they would collect their pre-school children at the end of the day and watch the elder sibling set off walking to catch the bus or train, or a combination of both, perhaps even changing trains, and maybe combined with a long walk navigating busy roads. It was only then that the significance of this issue hit home, that I realized that it was a rite of passage that in the end was nonnegotiable. As a British mother, I equate it with a parent handing over the car keys to a teenage child for the first time, knowing as they do so that they themselves will not sleep that night, nor perhaps any night, until they hear the child's key in the door.

Kye's father, with his Iranian background, takes a

similar view to my own, unable to conceive of letting our six-year-old walk to school alone. At the same time, he acknowledges the need for Kye to feel independent, and encourages me to remain in the background, an unobtrusive but necessary presence. If I were Japanese, this might be possible, but being a 5' 8" tall clumsy-looking Western woman I have yet to find a way of blending into the scenery. My husband recalls how, as a child in Iran, even once he reached an age when he was capable of going to school by himself, his mother continued to covertly follow him from a distance for many years to come, cloaked in a black chador and blending into a sea of other women cloaked in black chadors. I am not sure how much he exaggerates this story for comical effect, though given the fact that he was the long-awaited only brother of an only sister twelve years his senior, it is a likely scenario. In Iran today, in the cities at least, middle-class children would certainly be accompanied to school, while children from working-class backgrounds would be more likely to make their own way. It should be remembered, too, that some young children go out to work to bring in income for their families, so do not go to school at all.

The contrast between the practice in Japan and that in the U.K. and Australia at least is sharp. There, it is not only usual but often required that parents or caregivers accompany children to school, at least until around age nine or ten. The problems occur when someone challenges this thinking, as highlighted by a recent U.K. newspaper article. One mother decided that it would help foster her daughter's self-reliance if she were allowed to walk alone to school each day and that, since the route was one frequented by lots of children walking with their parents to the same school, the risks were absolutely minimal. However, the school informed the parents that it was unacceptable to allow the child to walk by herself, and that if the parents were too busy to take her then she should be ferried by taxi each day. The mother was unable to appreciate how her daughter would be safer in a taxi with a "stranger" (driver) than walking by herself among other children and parents from the same school. The school refused to budge on the issue, and she had no choice but to resume walking with her daughter to school.

While I appreciate the need children have to fit in with their peer group, I believe that the issue is somewhat more complex in a multicultural context such as ours. As non-Japanese parents who are fluent and literate in the Japanese language, the language of our son's peers, and increasingly the language of choice for Kye himself, I am becoming increasingly convinced that this only serves to blur the boundaries of identity in the mind of our child—both his own identity, and his perception of his parents' identity, thus exacerbating the difficulty he has in accepting why we feel the need to do things differently from the mainstream.

With the likelihood of our remaining in Japan until Kye is around nine years old, it is clear that a part of his identity will forever be bound up with Japan. In this sense, I believe that as a mother I will continue to face cross-cultural issues that stem from this time in our lives long after we have physically separated from that culture. Eventually, I anticipate that there will be a shift of focus to the culture of Iran within the mainstream of Australia. Only one aspect will remain constant, and that is the fluidity of our cultural boundaries, with all the challenges it entails and the endless scope it offers us for a global perspective.

Multicultural Lessons
by Michele Corkery

"Aiiy don't see nooo muff-ins," my six-year-old daughter says to me as she peers over the balcony above the café in the mezzanine of our condominium building. Her voice rises and falls with each word. It is nearly two years ago and we are waiting for the bus that will take her to kindergarten at her new school in an inner city neighborhood of Boston.

"What?" I say as I turn to look at her.

"Aiiy don't see nooo muff-ins," she says again, but this time I see her right hand is poised as if it is a gun.

"I think you're right," I say, staring at her now, the grin spreading across her face. "The muffins are still in the oven." I pause. "You know though. The proper way to say that is 'I don't see *any* muffins.' That's the way we talk. You know that, right?"

"Yah, I know," she says as she mouths the words again, her finger accenting them in the air. She turns her head and doesn't think I see that she begins to smile again.

When Isabel started at her new school, I expected her to come home and talk about the girls in her class with names like Arianna and Anna, and I was pleasantly surprised when she told me instead that her new best friends were Jahai and Angel, two of the black boys in her class. But with that simple exchange on a crisp fall morning, my daughter unknowingly forced me to come to terms with my own lack of exposure to the black culture.

My daughter Isabel is a white kid in an inner city school in Boston's Chinatown neighborhood. It's an inner city school but it happens to be one of the best public schools in Massachusetts. At least this is what the administration tells us when we attend parent nights and when they want us to donate money. And *Boston Magazine* did rate it #23 in its 2005 top 100 schools in Massachusetts issue, beating out affluent suburban schools to where many white city parents, with enough money, move when their kids turn five.

It's not as if my daughter is as white as I am, with blond hair and pale chicken-like skin that reveals the blue veins underneath. My husband is a first-generation Portuguese American, and Isabel has his olive skin that tans to a dark brown after the first few days of summer. But in the school's eyes she is still very much Caucasian when put next to the Asian, Black and Hispanic kids who fill the majority of the seats in the school.

On the first day in her new classroom, I automatically scanned the faces of the children—looking for ones who resembled my daughter's. There was one Caucasian boy and two half-Caucasian, half-Chinese girls. My daughter was a minority among minorities, and although this is what we had chosen for her, I was anxious. We'd moved her from the cushy Montessori School in one of the wealthiest neighborhoods in Boston where they gave scholarships to a few kids from more disadvantaged neighborhoods. Many of the children in the Montessori school had olive and brown skin too but they were immigrants from places like Saudi Arabia,

Dubai and Pakistan. Some of them had 24-hour nannies and stay-at-home mothers who picked them up from school with arms loaded with shopping bags from Neiman Marcus and Louis Vuitton.

Since my daughter's new school has a 70% Asian population (given its excellent reputation and location in the heart of Chinatown) some parents don't think it is diverse enough. A neighborhood artist whose son is also at the school tells me, "I've always wanted my son to be a minority but I wish there was a bigger variety of ethnic backgrounds."

My husband and I didn't necessarily have this same wish for our child, although we supported the idea of Isabel learning in a multicultural setting. And we didn't move our daughter to the public school because my husband was an art teacher in a public inner city school or because we were only committed to a public education. Our decision wasn't so noble. It was the economics that finally won out. With my part-time job as an account executive in a communications agency and my husband's school teacher's salary, we just couldn't afford the "independent" school tuition another year. If we'd had more money or had our parents' financial help (like many of our friends at the Montessori school did), we may have kept our daughter at the school where kids wear slippers in class and can have their snack whenever they choose, even though we weren't entirely sure how we felt about the education she was getting.

When we saw the tuition bill for my daughter's kindergarten year at the Montessori school, we put the school in Chinatown at the top of our wish list and crossed our fingers that Boston's lottery system would work in our favor. We felt comfortable with the predominantly Asian population, due to our own biases. As a public school teacher in a neighboring city, my husband often marvels at how disciplined and polite his Asian students are. He says of all the students he's had (close to 500 each year for the past 12 years), only once has he had to severely discipline an Asian student. Meanwhile he's had many issues with kids from other ethnic backgrounds (including Caucasian kids)—one threw a chair at him, one stole from his classroom, and numerous others have verbally threatened him. Isabel's new school promoted the Asian stereotype. Its students were hard working, self controlled, and taught to be respectful of their teachers and parents; the families, including the extended families, had high expectations and were involved in their children's educations. I trusted that the Asian kids would be serious about school.

By sending Isabel to the school in Chinatown, my husband and I had consciously rejected another well-regarded public school that was in the Dorchester section of Boston and half of whose student population was black. Isabel had initially gotten into this school and was put on the waiting list at the Chinatown one. I was relieved when Isabel finally got into our first-choice school, partly because getting to Dorchester would have been a much longer commute from our downtown neighborhood and partly because I wasn't entirely sure how comfortable I felt sending Isabel to a school where half of its students were black. My hesitancy was influenced by the *New York Times* articles I'd read highlighting the widening gap between black and Hispanic students and their white and Asian contemporaries, and my limited exposure to the black culture also made the Asian culture seem more inviting.

Yet, when Isabel started school in Chinatown, I didn't realize that it would be her interactions with the black children at the school that would dominate her initial awareness of race and force me to consider my own racial biases. Her first friend in kindergarten was the largest boy in her class, an expressive black child who would hug me each time I picked her up at the end of the school day and who was often asked to sit in the "time out" chair. One of her other "best friends" turned out to be a mild-mannered black boy with beaming brown eyes and a quiet smile. Isabel didn't like the two black girls in her class, complaining that when one of them was chosen to be her partner for the month, she wouldn't hold Isabel's hand when they walked through the hallways, like she was supposed to do.

I remember the first time I had lunch with Isabel in the separate room of the cafeteria that was reserved for the kindergartners. About ten minutes after lunch started, Jahai was up, sliding back and forth along the linoleum in his slippery-soled sneakers. Isabel watched him and laughed at him until the lunch monitor told him firmly to take his seat. He rolled his eyes and Isabel laughed again. When she saw me looking at her, my eyebrows furled, she averted her gaze and began whispering to the friend sitting next to her.

My parents moved out of the city when the busing started in the Boston area in the early 1970s. We moved to a mostly white suburb on the South Shore where there were three black kids and one Jewish kid in my class. I don't remember any Asian children in the town.

My parents always said they had "no problem with black or Asian people." They had even considered adopting a child from Vietnam after the war ended. But all of their friends were white.

When I was a child, my parents and I would often ride through Massachusetts Avenue in Roxbury to cross over to Cambridge (where my parents grew up and my grandparents still lived), and my parents always told me to lock my door once we got off the exit. I was afraid but curious as I peered out the windows at dark faces in the streets and in the cars around us. Most days, no one even looked our way, but one afternoon a black man casually banged his fist on the hood of our car when we were stopped at a light. He looked as if he was on his way somewhere and we simply crossed his path.

Once Isabel started at her new school, I became acutely aware of my own lack of experience with the black culture. Through her, I saw an opportunity for me to better understand and make some connection with black people. I enthusiastically encouraged her friendships with the one black girl whose mother also picked up her daughter from school rather than having her take the bus home. It may sound naïve but I also wanted to have a black friend.

At the first parents' night, I left my new white and Asian friends to talk with the black parents. I later tried to get to know all of the children in Isabel's classroom by visiting when I could, and I made an extra effort to reach out to the black children. I read with them and sat with them while they finished their arts and crafts projects.

I visited Isabel's classroom one Friday when they were studying weather. They had to construct a class quilt made from their individual weather collages, and I helped one of the black girls in her class glue clouds made from cotton balls onto the blue construction paper. "Do you ever look at the clouds and imagine that they are shaped like different animals?" I asked her. She smiled at me knowingly but was too shy to tell me what animals she had seen in the clouds until I told her I had once imagined an elephant with a long trunk and big floppy ears. "A bunny," she said excitedly and she placed her wrists on her beaded head, her fingers pointing up, to create bunny ears.

On the rare occasion that I would see one of the black children's parents at pickup, I would smile, try to make small talk, or share some lame observation about their son or daughter as if I had some sort of relationship with their kids. "Jahai is getting so tall," I'd say. "Jeysaun is such a sweet boy." I didn't want the black parents to think I was one of those bigoted white women who crossed the street at night when a black man was in her path. Or maybe I just wanted to prove to myself that I wasn't.

I began to choose the grocery store lines that had black cashiers and struck up conversations with the black cab drivers I came into contact with. I became more aware of the thoughts I had when a young black man walked too slowly through a busy intersection when it wasn't his right of way to cross. I didn't like that my mind immediately made a connection between the black man crossing the street and an anti-establishment, anti-white attitude. I wanted to change the generalizations I was making, not only on the streets but in the classroom. For example, I remember being surprised to see that the child with the most discipline problems in Isabel's kindergarten classroom was a white boy and not being surprised when the other boy with discipline problems was a black.

I also began to realize that the Asian kids were not such a homogenous group. Sure, there were a number who fit the stereotypes, but there were quite a few who had behavioral issues that could challenge even the most competent teacher. I started to analyze my thoughts about culture and race more readily, realizing this would be the first step in changing automatic associations that I didn't like. I didn't feel as if I was doing enough, but I was finally beginning to venture out from the confines of my relatively white world.

My daughter is finishing up first grade at the school in Chinatown. She has many friends, and while her choices in friends still appear to be color blind, they seem to be fairly rigid when it comes to sex, socio-economic class and education level. Her closest friends' are all girls now and their parents are small-business owners, college professors, businessmen and women, and directors at non-profit companies. Isabel likes her new school, particularly the playground on the roof, although she still thinks wistfully of her days in the "more comfty" (her words, not mine) Montessori school.

This year she studied the Civil Rights Movement and brought home a book about Ruby Bridges, the little girl who was the first black student to attend an all-white school in New Orleans in 1960. As she read the story to me and told me how black children used to be treated, she looked at me in disbelief as she said, "You know Mommy. If we still lived when black and white children weren't allowed to go to school together, Kamaiya, Tahliyaa and Jeysaun wouldn't be in my classroom. And they're all so nice." She continued with tears welling in her eyes. "Can you believe that? We wouldn't even be allowed to drink from the same water fountain!"

This exchange made me feel proud that my daughter was in a school that my parents have said resembles the "United Nations." It always strikes me how white all of the faces are in the class photographs that are taped to the refrigerators at my friends' houses in the suburbs. If Isabel was attending a school that was mostly white, she would likely still study the same Civil Rights Movement lesson, but she wouldn't have such direct exposure to so many black children. She would be able to see the injustice of racism but the concept would remain abstract. Because of her experiences, Isabel is able to personalize racism in a way that many of my friends' children cannot and that I could not at her age.

Still, there's a part of me that understands why Isabel tries to pull me to the next train car when she sees a group of young black men in baggy jeans and too-long T-shirts pushing and shoving on the car that we are waiting to board. A group of teenagers can be intimidating and we've come across many of these groups in the inner city, kids of all different ethnic backgrounds. They are often too loud, crass and bold; they can make me feel uncomfortable too.

I take Isabel's hand and board the same train car the kids are riding. Isabel stares at the kids who are now swearing at one another; her eyes dart back and forth from them to me.

"I wouldn't want to be a black boy," Isabel says to me later when we are walking home from the subway.

"Why do you say that?" I ask.

"They think they're so cool," she says. "I don't want to be cool. I want to be fashion."

At first, I begin to worry that perhaps this is some sort of prejudice against blacks coming through, even after her all of her exposure to different ethnic groups. I play out the conversation I will have with her later about not judging people based on the color of their skin. And then I realize that my reaction is more about my judgments, not hers. I am projecting onto her my fears about some deep-rooted racism that I am afraid I harbor but am not fully aware of. It is then that I realize that Isabel is responding appropriately to what has just occurred. She is not afraid to speak out loud against something or someone who makes her uncomfortable, whatever their race. Even though she has generalized in her language about not wanting to be a black boy, her comment is really about not wanting to be a particular kind of boy, one she is threatened by.

I decide it is best to let her comment go and allow her to decide for herself how she will interact with kids of other ethnic backgrounds. Already, she has more experience than I.

A Santa Snafu
by Kathy Hamilton

Being the lone foreign parent in a school can be lonely, as I discovered last December 26. When I dropped my son off at his kindergarten the other mothers, who were usually warm to me, suddenly seemed to regard me as an enemy. No friendly greetings met me that morning, and no small talk. I wondered what Ali Adem, my son, had done this time. So far, he had navigated his dual cultural heritage fairly easily, but I was always on the lookout for potential problems between his American and Turkish cultures and traditions.

Living in Istanbul, the cosmopolitan center of Turkey, straddling both Europe and Asia, had not posed any major problems at the start for my Turkish husband and me, a transplanted Texan by way of Washington DC. However, when our son, Ali Adem, was born, my husband and I found ourselves having to learn the ins and outs of raising a child in two cultures. I had studied Islam and converted to Islam on my first trip to Turkey in 1981. We decided to raise our son as a Muslim, but to make sure he knew and respected all other religious traditions, including those of my Christian family living in the United States.

Before our son started school, we traveled together to South Texas to spend the Thanksgiving and Christmas holidays with my mother. Each visit was anxiously awaited as Ali Adem learned to mark off the days before departure on the wall calendar in his room. Once in San Antonio, we would help my mother decorate her apartment, and it would soon be filled with a blend of American and Mexican influences as Nat King Cole, Bing Crosby and mariachi music filled the air with festive melodies. A small, decorated tree perched in a corner, with piles of gifts scattered underneath it. On the dining room table was the family *nacimiento*—a hand-made Nativity scene from the Mexican village of Oaxaca. For his first five years, Ali Adem was sure that Santa knew his Nana's address and would not forget him on his yearly trip around the world.

Once he started kindergarten at a local Turkish school, our yearly Christmas holiday visits to my mother's home ceased because the Turkish school system schedules the winter break the first two weeks of February and not at the end of December. Although Turkey is a secular country, the vast majority of Turks are Muslim, and many are not familiar with Christian traditions or celebrations. Ali Adem does not know all the religious symbolism of the yuletide season, but he does know that it is a time of year to be with family, think about others, give gifts to those you love, and share with those less fortunate. Thanks in part to the movie *The Polar Express*, he also knows about Santa and each year he anxiously awaits his visits from the North Pole. He is also proud of the fact that like him, St. Nick is from Turkey, something he loves to inform often-surprised Americans when we travel to my home country.

Many people do not know that the history behind the legend of Saint Nicholas lies in what is now Turkey. Around 271 AD Nicholas was born in Patara, near Myra, modern day

Demre, in Asia Minor. Eventually he rose to the rank of bishop of the church and was known for his acts of kindness towards the poor and sick. In one story, he is said to have saved three young girls from being sold into slavery by their desperately poor family who could not afford the required dowry in order to marry them off. Upon hearing this news, Nicholas gathered together gold coins into three small sacks. Late at night, he quietly went to the family's humble home, and tossed the bags down the chimney, where they landed in the cold embers of the fireplace. The next morning, the family awoke and rejoiced in the good fortune that had saved their daughters and now enabled them to marry into good families. In recent years, as Western customs become more global, the figure of St. Nicholas has begun to appear throughout Turkey, but as a symbol of the New Year. Small Turkish children know him as a thin man, dressed in a red coat, bearing gifts to celebrate the arrival of a new year. Just before New Year's Eve, decorations are strung in many homes and some families decorate a fir tree, all reminiscent of Christmas holidays in other countries.

This year, however, as Christmas approached, Ali Adem realized that we would not be at his Nana's house for the holiday season and he worried that the jolly old man might not know where to find him. But, after I reassured him that he would not be overlooked in Turkey, he began counting down the days and planning what kind of cookies would go best with the milk we would leave out for Santa and his reindeer. On Christmas Eve he carefully positioned the plate and cup of frothy milk on the living room table, assured that St. Nick would be able to spot them. For good measure he wrote a note saying "For Santa" with an arrow pointing towards the plate. Satisfied, he excitedly snuggled into his bed for the night.

Early the next morning I was awakened by him jumping on the bed, arms laden with carefully wrapped presents he had found in the living room, piled high next to the empty plate and glass. "Santa came!" he yelled as he bounced while waving his packages, "I just know he brought me everything I wanted!" As I began breakfast he spread out his new stash of toys, books and clothes across the living room floor. Reminding him that he still had to go to school even though it was Christmas Day, he reluctantly got dressed, ate his morning meal and got prepared to leave for the day. Wistfully eyeing his new gifts displayed in our home, as we left, he said, "Mommy, what do you think the other kids in my class got from Santa?"

It was not until that moment that I realized, with a sinking feeling in my stomach, that we might have a potential problem on our hands since all his classmates are Turkish, and I was fairly certain that none of them would have received any gifts that morning. I tried to explain as we walked the two blocks to school that his friends did not know about Santa, and therefore they would not have gotten presents, as he had. Puzzled, he asked, "But, were they bad? Is that why Santa didn't bring them gifts? He was Turkish, and so are they, so they should know all about him." Seeing the logic of his thoughts, I attempted to clarify the situation, saying that it was not a matter of his friends misbehaving during the year that caused them to miss out on the holiday. Instead, since they did not know about St. Nick and the traditions we practiced at home, he did not stop by their houses. I pleaded with him not to brag about his windfall to his classmates since that might make them feel left out. Nodding in agreement, he kissed me and skipped off into his classroom.

Returning to pick him up that afternoon from school, I was surrounded by a loud cluster of his classmates, all tugging on me, vying for my attention and demanding to know why they had not had a visit from Santa the night before. After getting the children to quiet down, I discovered that they had heard about Ali Adem's midnight visit from Santa and they all demanded to know why they had not been on his checklist also. Trying to reassure them that I did not have any special insider connection with the jolly man, I struggled for a way to explain to them in my very fractured Turkish that this was not a custom widely celebrated here, and that was probably why they had not gotten any gifts. At that point, Ali Adem chimed in, haughtily saying that only good children received presents, and therefore, they all must have been very terrible to merit not a single gift. Disagreeing loudly with his pronouncement, the children clamored for clarification. "What! I was too good! Ali Adem behaved worse than me, so I should get his gifts!" the voices howled in protest as I tried to pry myself and my son from the tiny mob before things got ugly. Grasping his hand, I pulled him with me to the door as I extracted small children clutching at my clothes, still demanding explanations.

That evening Ali Adem and I sat together in his bed and talked about his day. Still puzzled, he asked, "Why were my friends so upset about me getting presents? Sometimes they get presents for Turkish holidays and it doesn't bother me. Will they still be my friends tomorrow?" Hoping that this would be a storm that passed quickly, I replied, "Well, sweetie, I think they were upset because you told them that they didn't get presents because they were bad. Not everyone believes in Santa like we do. That doesn't mean they are bad, though. I'm sure your friends will still like you and play with you. But, maybe tomorrow you should try really hard to not mention anything about all your gifts." As he snuggled under his blankets he grudgingly agreed to my request and I hoped for the best.

It was not until the next day, however, that the full impact of Christmas Day hit me, as some of the mothers ignored my greetings and turned away from me when we dropped off our children for school on that cold, wintery morning. Since they had always been very pleasant and welcoming to me before, I suspected that their sudden change in attitude was due to the Santa incident the previous day. Wanting to try to soothe any ruffled feathers, I pulled Betul aside to explain. Previously she had made a point of taking me under her wing to make sure that I understood all the school procedures and events. Speaking in my child-like Turkish, I struggled for words that were quickly slipping from my mind in an attempt to make things right with everyone. "Please, don't be mad. I'm sorry. Yesterday Ali Adem got gifts. In America, yesterday important day. My family not here. Ali Adem and I happy for Christmas together. Santa come and Ali Adem excited. Not want to be mean to his friends. We don't mean to make the children unhappy. But, my family not here and it important day," I spluttered out, close to tears, hoping that she could somehow understand what I meant.

Listening, Betul nodded. She then turned to the other mothers who were clustered nearby, listening to me speak. "She is right, she has no family here. How would we feel if we lived in another country, struggled with the language, and had our holidays all by ourselves? We should make allowances for her," she said to the gathered group. "I really don't think they meant for all our children to get so upset. How could she know? Besides, we have holidays that we celebrate that she doesn't know anything about. We give our children candy and gifts at the end of Ramadan, but that is not a custom in America. Maybe it's good for our own children to learn about other cultures," she added as the other mothers paused in thought. Slowly their heads nodded in agreement as they accepted that I had not meant to slight their own children by allowing my son to celebrate a day that was important to us, and was a part of his American heritage. Accepting my apologies, we parted in good spirits.

When I returned to the school later that afternoon to pick up Ali Adem, I spoke with his teacher and explained the reaction of the other mothers. She understood the significance of the holiday for me and my son, and she told me that the usual New Year's program at the school should solve our problems. "Don't worry," she said, "they will forget all about it soon enough."

The following week a costume party was held for all the kindergarten students in celebration of the upcoming New Year. After games had been played and cake served, the highlight of the festivities arrived—a thin man, dressed in a red suit trimmed with white fake fur, with a bag slung over his shoulder. Noel Baba, the Turkish version of Santa, had arrived right on schedule, much to the children's delight. "Happy New Year!" he announced and from his large bag he pulled out a gaily-wrapped New Year's present for every child. As his classmates were delighted to know that they too had been visited by Santa, albeit a few days later than Ali Adem, any hard feelings they still harbored vanished as the party ended and everyone headed home.

Two Versions of Immersion
by Holly Thompson

Ten years ago this summer, we left the Hudson River town where we'd recently bought a home, uprooting our small children from their friends and extended family for a new life in Japan. A job had been offered to my husband in Tokyo, and since times were slow in New York and I needed to finish my novel that was set in Japan, we thought a change was in order. What's more, we'd missed living overseas. How perfect, we thought, to have the chance to raise our children bilingually. How thrilling to be able to offer them the language immersion experience.

We sold the house, recouped enough to fund the move and buy a few pieces of furniture for our Japanese rental home. International schooling, housing and all those expat goodies were not part of the new job arrangement; rather we were flown over, allowed to ship only basics and given a small housing allowance—like an employee coming to Tokyo from Hokkaido, the firm's personnel department explained. We would have to make do like a Japanese family. This suited us fine and fit well with our immersion goals: to settle in a Japanese neighborhood and plunge ourselves into the local community.

Some in New York criticized the move as cruel to our children. Others met our news with delight—a place abroad to visit. A few sympathized with the enormous changes we faced. But no one was more daunted than me—my husband would be engrossed in his new job over an hour's commute from our home, and I would be the parent to carry the better part of the burden of creating two bilingual children from scratch.

Because my husband and I had lived in Japan early in our marriage and had both taught in Japanese public schools, we thought we knew what we were getting into. We both had Japanese skills, his more developed than mine, and we believed our children would do fine in local Japanese pre- and elementary schools. We felt equipped to offer them the support they would need. For middle school, some years away, we would consider international schools, but for starters, we were committed to immersing our children in Japan's public education system.

We arrived in mid-August and tried to acclimate. A seven-year-old understands at least fundamentally what it is to move overseas, what it means to face a year without going back to old friends and family and what is required to converse in another language: our son tackled kanji eagerly, studied hard to memorize grammar, did his best to communicate with neighborhood children and seemed destined for success. Our active two-year-old daughter, on the other hand, thought a week in Japan was plenty, thank you very much, then was fed up with children in the park who didn't respond to her chatter, language that made no sense, and people who didn't know her. We had an angry, resentful child who felt trapped thousands of miles from the backyards where she wanted to be.

Our son soon started the fall term of grade two at the

local elementary school. He was the first ever child of two non-Japanese parents to attend. The administration was nervous about us, but we reiterated our enthusiasm for helping our son adjust and explained that we'd already taught him first-grade kana and kanji and had started second-grade kanji. We would do everything we could to make the transition as smooth as possible, we assured them, and we looked forward to becoming part of the school community. They relaxed. Then we asked what sort of support the school would provide to a second-language learner such as our son. "If you'd like, we can arrange for a volunteer to visit the classroom once a week," replied the principal. We thought we'd misheard. A volunteer? Once a week? But we'd heard right.

Discouraged, but resigned, I made arrangements to meet our son and his teacher after school every day to note important vocabulary from the day, do my best to translate between them and help clear any misunderstandings. The teacher soon made it clear that once a week was as much time as she could spare. The full extent of government second-language support therefore boiled down to these brief meetings and a once-a-week classroom visit from a community volunteer. We wondered what happened to children of immigrants whose parents couldn't speak Japanese. At least we could help our son with his homework. At least we could read, with the aid of dictionaries, the handouts sent home from the school. And at least we could afford to hire a private tutor for our son.

Fortunately within six months our son was linguistically functional; by the end of second grade he was at grade level for kanji, and he could manage in the classroom on his own. In language, therefore, his immersion was proving a success. However, the chaos in the classroom astounded him and us. The teacher was kind enough, but she had no control over the students. Kids regularly hit each other. They ran wild through corridors. They menaced each other during cleaning time. Our son was hit hard on the head by peers—whenever he made a mistake. The teacher observed and did nothing. "Children need freedom," "Children need to learn to resolve their own problems," were the catch phrases. And so at our local Japanese school, children did resolve their own problems—through bullying and physical abuse of weaker and outwardly different children...such as our son.

Our son longed for English-language peers and fun, invigorating classes. He wept to recall his teachers, friends and calm classrooms in New York. Soon an acquaintance introduced us to an aikido dojo, and that became the nurturing Japanese environment that helped our son remember that he was strong and worthwhile, and helped remind us in our lowest moments that the negative school environment was not culture-wide. Aikido and a weekend nature program introduced him to different sorts of peers and strong, caring Japanese teachers and leaders.

Meanwhile I was taking our daughter to various pre-preschool programs, trying to help her adapt to new types of play circles and new ways of communication. We learned songs, play motions, proper ways to greet people, seasonal markers and celebrations, how to make and eat *bento* lunches, how to wait patiently for an event to happen and then wait for it to finish...all the foundations of a Japanese education. Yet she was frustrated by lack of language ability. She was a spirited, physical child, and formal language tutoring was out of the question. So we did our best to introduce her to Japanese vocabulary and phrases. We used mostly Japanese outside the house and a mix of Japanese and English at home. Some professionals might fault this hodge-podge method, but our daughter needed Japanese to participate in play circles and park activities. She needed words to enable her to be the interactive child she clearly wanted to be. She needed words to staunch her anger. So we fed her Japanese vocabulary daily. We refrained when she was moody, and we had to compartmentalize our teachings so as not to confuse her, but she definitely needed both Japanese and English language development from us.

We spent an inordinate amount of money on shipping books in those days—pre-Amazon Japan—and we spent much time in the local Japanese library. Our aim was to enable both children to catch up to their peers in Japan and keep them equal academically to their peers in the U.S. This required considerable supplemental work at home, especially for two children five years apart with vastly different personalities and different academic and developmental needs. I was required to play teacher in both languages. I also had to further develop my own skills in Japanese so that I could manage in parent-teacher conferences, participate in open classroom days and have regular conversations with other parents. Some days I was triumphant having successfully written a note to a teacher, or navigated a clinic visit, or solved some long math word problems. Other days I was vocabulary numb, unable to absorb another word, unable to recall peoples' names and exhausted by even a simple shopping task in Japanese.

Fortunately soon after arriving in Japan we joined an English-language playgroup that developed into a learning circle; participants included other English-speaking children who attended Japanese public pre- and elementary schools around the region. Through this group we met international families and families like ours with no Japanese blood. Our children developed lasting friendships and resurrected their battered self-esteems. This cooperative learning circle continued for years, offering many area children a supportive environment in which to learn with peers in English as parents took turns teaching units on science, geography, history, music, art and more. Our kids gained self-confidence and developed a clear sense of identity as bicultural children.

Our daughter started Japanese preschool (*yochien*) in April, eight months after our arrival in Japan. She was thrilled to set off the first day, proud of her uniform and delighted with the bus. When we woke her the second day though, she protested. "But I've been to *yochien*! I don't need to go again!" Somehow, we'd failed to convey that it would be a daily occurrence—Monday to Friday and two Saturdays a month. The first term of *yochien* certainly provided her with intense and effective language immersion, but the experience exhausted her. What's more, I started university teaching, so that several days a week she attended extended hours. The *yochien* teachers were kind, superhumanly energetic and much adored, but with thirty-five children in a classroom, there was little individual attention.

Everything hinged on working with the group, on being like the group in behavior, words and appearance. Even though by Japanese standards this *yochien* was relaxed, many days our young daughter raged against herself for not fitting in, not being enough like the other children.

After a year in Japan we made our first trip back to the U.S. The kids were reunited with friends and family and re-immersed into the world they had been so comfortable in before our move; conversations were easy, social situations were a breeze, life seemed simple. Returning to Japan some weeks later was difficult; hearing and speaking Japanese required continuous effort; there seemed to be rules for everything. The children settled back into their school routines with a sense of resignation.

Our son continued to make great strides in Japanese during his second year; to his embarrassment, his teacher held up his strong kanji tests in an attempt to shame his classmates into improving. He could now handle most class- and homework with just a few hours of support from me per week. But course content was dull; students were not allowed to tackle more challenging math problems until all children in the class had mastered a concept; the same science test would be given three times until the material was learned; and history and geography—two of our son's favorite subjects—were not taught in the lower grades. To top it off the teacher was ill, missed many days of school and slept in class, and when he was absent, no substitute was called in. Other teachers looked in on the class, set the students work to do, then left; classroom chaos intensified. Even today, many years later, our son finds it difficult to talk about the daily verbal and physical abuses he endured that year. He did have a group of good friends, but even they were not enough to offset his misery.

Our daughter made steady gains, and by April of her second year of *yochien* she was full of linguistic confidence. She now loved extended-hour days when I had work; there were fewer children than in the regular classroom, and with afterschool teachers they took walks, harvested seasonal fruits or vegetables, cooked, did crafts and played outside. She was becoming a happier child.

That same April our son advanced into fourth grade. This boy who had always been an ardent learner had grown utterly bored with school—he was coping but cynical and unexcited. No matter how much supplementing we did at home, we could not offset the fact that he spent hour after uninspired hour at the local elementary school. To make matters worse, after the third-grade teacher who'd been absent much of the year, we'd thought any fourth-grade teacher would be an improvement. But our son landed a teacher famous in the district for her monotonous talk. By then our son was highly critical of his Japanese elementary school experience; we knew a year with this teacher would prove disastrous. We looked into moving. We thought of homeschooling. We had to do something; we were losing our once highly motivated child. Finally we used all our savings, borrowed money and put him in an international school—where he immediately thrived.

It was tempting to view his immersion experience as a failure, and it was on some levels. His Japanese school experience proved a profound disappointment both academically and socially, and, sadly, once he moved out of the elementary school, he did not maintain close contact with his few good friends. But the language skills acquired in the Japanese elementary school experience served him well as he took native-level Japanese classes at the international school and other language classes through middle school and high school. With regained confidence he took on major leadership roles. He loved learning with other bicultural and tricultural students who could think on a global scale, and he kept one foot firmly planted in the local Japanese community through aikido, music lessons, volunteer work at a local nature preserve and participation in annual festivals.

Our daughter's trajectory has been different. Equipped with the social tools acquired in three years of *yochien,* and fully bilingual when she began at the same local Japanese elementary school that our son attended, she was poised for a different experience. Fortunately, some of the teachers had been shaken out of the system by then, and in our daughter's six years of elementary school, she only had one year of what we called chaos—and at least that chaos was fun, including hours of unstructured play time at the beach. She also had what our son had lacked in his immersion experience: a close friend in the neighborhood. Our daughter and her friend walked to school together every day and played together afterward. They ate dinner at each others' houses, and as their friendship developed, so did the friendship between her mother and myself. Our daughter's Japanese improved by leaps and bounds thanks to this family. Also in her grade level were several children with a non-Japanese parent—one of whom spoke English. In addition, newcomers from other parts of Japan were moving into our seaside town; overall attitudes of parents and teachers were therefore more open and welcoming to differences than in our son's days there. Our daughter did suffer her share of bullying taunts: "Die, alien!" "We should have beat you in the war, idiot!" "Stupid foreigner," and more, but with the support of close friends she coped, and she never suffered the physical blows that our son did.

We had every intention of having our daughter graduate from her Japanese elementary school. She was fond of her teachers, had many friends and had undertaken leadership roles in the upper grades. Yet although the Japanese school experience for her had been largely positive, she had much ground to make up in English if she hoped to succeed in the international school's middle and high school. We also wanted her to overlap with her brother during his last year at the international school. Our daughter therefore left her Japanese school midway through the Japanese academic year to start sixth grade at the international school.

Over the past year, she has struggled to adjust to reading and writing in English, and she has missed her former peers, but she has loved her new school experience. She tends to favor Japanese-speaking friends, continues to read novels in Japanese, and though her reading and writing of Japanese has dropped below her peers in her Japanese school, she is more completely bilingual than anyone else in our family. Having been raised almost entirely in Japan within the Japanese education system, Japanese values inform her actions and attitude, and people often comment that she seems like a Japanese packaged in a non-Japanese body.

We've learned that each individual child and each set of circumstances will yield a unique result from language immersion. Our self-assurance and naiveté when we first arrived with our children has been replaced with a deep understanding of bilingualism and of the challenges facing all migrants who don't speak the local language. Success depends on far more than vocabulary acquisition.

This month, our son sets off for his first year at university in New York City, ten years after moving to Japan at age seven. He is daunted by the move, unsure how it will feel to live in the U.S. again and anxious to meet other international students during university orientation. He knows he will deeply miss this country where he has been raised; he knows he will feel out of place in the city of his birth. He has made his sister promise to e-mail him in Japanese. And, while we look forward to visiting him mid-term at home in the States, we especially look forward to winter break when we can welcome him back "home" here in Japan.

I am Mutti
by Corey Heller

Germany is a country located in Central Europe, between France and Denmark, Poland and the Netherlands. Its culture and language stretch far and wide, even as far as the hearts and minds of my three young children living in America. Although they are still oblivious to it, my children will always be tied to two countries separated by an ocean. American and German: the two intertwine neatly yet independently in my family, along blurred lines of language, culture and identity.

In 1991 I boarded a plane for Galway, Ireland. I had never traveled to another country for any period of time (other than family winter vacations to Mexico, bouncing along the roads in our VW Bus), let alone lived in one thousands of miles away from family and friends. Yet, deep down inside I had the feeling that my year abroad in Ireland would change my life completely and permanently. And that it did. Living in Ireland sobered me to the fact that the world is a big, big place and that my customs and traditions had limited use while living abroad. My American accent, which was commonplace on my home soil, was the embodiment of an entire cultural stereotype while standing on the soil of another.

Returning to California after my year in Ireland, I experienced what experts call Reverse Culture Shock. To me it felt like a kind of cultural purgatory of my own making. I realized that I'd never be able to go back home again; at least not completely. The consequences of assimilating to a surrounding culture are that we run the risk of depending upon bits of it for our sense of self and belonging. Those which at first are the strangest and most dissimilar to our own culture slowly weave their way into our being until we have forgotten what we were before. And then it is too late.

While living in Ireland I met Rainer, a blond-haired, cheerful, intelligent young student from northern Germany. Neither of us was interested in a relationship with the other, perhaps in part due to our respective cultures. It's not that I had anything against Germans. I didn't really know anything about them. And Rainer, in his own right, was not particularly interested in a relationship with an American. So, although we had some of the best conversations ever and delighted in each other's company, we were still quite safe from anything more than random bits of friendship and silly flirtations. At least that is what we told ourselves back then.

Needless to say, we did end up together as our year in Ireland came to a close and we were forced to decide whether or not to continue our romance. I returned home to California, took a leave of absence from my university, packed my bags and in the fall headed to Kiel in northern Germany. I can still remember the sights and smells of that first day: damp autumn leaves scattered along brick sidewalks, the warm smiles of Rainer's parents as they greeted me that first time, the swiftness of the Autobahn and Rainer's tiny apartment lacking hot running water yet full of comfort and charm.

In Kiel, I spent five days a week in intensive German language classes with a teacher who was strict, serious, bulging pregnant with twins, and who never, ever spoke anything but German with us. She would check our homework daily and reprimand us if we either failed to do it or didn't do it properly. We were never allowed to look in a dictionary (we had to ask her in our broken German if we had any vocabulary questions) and we were strictly forbidden to use any language except German. The class itself was made up of students from all around the world: twenty-six individuals of all ages and twenty different native tongues.

The experience of living in a new country can feel overwhelming, especially when it includes learning a new language. It exhausts and incapacitates while at the same time exhilarating and fascinating. The inability to communicate or express myself during those early months in Germany made me feel like an infant learning her first words; trying out sentences, observing the response to each utterance. Jokes, in particular, were difficult: They were patiently translated to me as everyone waited in excited anticipation of my laughter, but I was often unable to completely grasp the meaning and thus the humor (and my response, despite great effort) fell short. And without the celebration of my traditional holidays to fall back upon, I sometimes felt isolated. People were delighted to learn about my traditions but holidays such as Thanksgiving came and went without the single sighting of a turkey.

One day I was purchasing goods in a store and after giving the cashier fifty marks, she only returned a ten mark bill plus some change. I went into a sudden internal panic. She should have returned a twenty mark bill plus change! I tried to tell her as much but I had not yet learned the past-tense in class. So, I stated, "You give me ten marks." But the tired, annoyed cashier just looked at me blankly and called the next person. I didn't budge. I kept trying to make myself understood, becoming breathless and turning bright red in the process. "You give me twenty marks, but you give me ten marks." It was hopeless. Finally, a kind gentleman behind me asked if I spoke English. Relieved, I explained the situation to him, he translated it for the cashier and I did get my correct change back (along with a very dirty look from the cashier). I felt small and insignificant. I felt like telling everyone, "I come from America. I am educated. I am not as tiny and stupid as it seems. I am like you!" But instead I said "*Danke,*" walked home and cried on Rainer's shoulder.

By the end of my second year in Germany (with a year in between when I completed my Bachelor's degree in California), I felt empowered. My cultural and linguistic deficiencies no longer held me captive. Finally steady on my linguistic footing, I was a willing and able sparring partner, relishing my ability to parry and dodge. I was even attending regular university courses at the Christian-Albrecht-Universitaet in Kiel.

Should I admit that I relished the opportunity of being someone special while in Germany? I was the resident American who had learned German. I was called upon to answer all questions about America and the English language. I was praised for having learned German so well, so accent-free. Family and friends who before had had to speak English with me were now conversing with me in German, something in which we all took great delight and which encouraged me to continue mastering the language. I felt elated. I felt wanted. I felt on top of the world.

In 1995 Rainer and I married and in the fall moved to the United States. During our first year in Seattle, Rainer and I each went through our own cultural assimilations. Rainer was fascinated with things that I took for granted: coupons for free items with mail-in rebates, political leaders who stated the United States was "number one" and endless religious channels preaching a variety of sermons. I, on the other hand, spent my first year back in the United States, pining for Germany, begging my husband to take me back to Kiel. I felt out of place in the US, like a foreigner in my own land. In time, however, we each slowly adapted to my native culture and learned to appreciate it; bit by bit becoming Americanized and gradually letting go of our German cultural expectations. We didn't even visit Germany those first few years (as a plane flight was expensive for young grad students) until my husband's father was diagnosed with kidney cancer in 1998.

There is something very disorienting about living abroad from a family member who has been diagnosed with a life-threatening disease. On the one hand, you feel helpless and hopeless. There is nothing you can do in that moment when you receive the news and you are left waiting and wondering, feeling isolated far away from family. Yet at the same time, you feel detached and distanced. As if nothing has changed, as if today is the same as yesterday and the world is all good and well. It isn't until your plane lands in the other country and your embraces with loved ones have taken place that the reality starts to set in. The voices, the holding of hands, the conversations face-to-face, they bring us to a kind of raw truth, one which cannot be avoided no matter the attempts.

Rainer flew back and forth to Germany during his father's year-long battle with kidney cancer. He spent many hours at his father's bedside, deep in conversation or just being present. He heard his father's regrets, his joys, his sorrows and delights. And one night, a few days after I had arrived and my father-in-law had looked into my eyes and said, "Now everyone is here," he passed away and was buried in the church graveyard near his parents' graves and where his wife will one day be buried.

In 2001, Patrick, our first child, was born.

I don't remember speaking much German to Patrick when he was an infant but perhaps I did. Either way, it just didn't seem like an issue and definitely didn't come up as a topic for discussion. It wasn't until my sister-in-law and her friend were visiting us (a few months after our second child, Christoph, was born) that my husband and I had "the talk." His sister had asked me if we intended to raise our children in German. Of course my husband would, but she wanted to know what my plans were. For the first time I asked my husband if he thought it was okay for me to speak German with our children as our home language. I felt it was ultimately his decision since if I were to mangle his language I could understand if he'd rather that I stick with my own native tongue. My husband was elated. He was delighted that I *wanted* to speak German with our children. And the truth is, I was relieved. I had felt a deep desire to speak German with our children, a desire which even to this day I don't completely understand. I acknowledge that it has much to do with my hard-won bonds with the German language and culture but I am certain that it has even deeper roots than I can traverse.

Some ask if I speak German with my children for my husband's sake. They wonder if I do it so that my husband will feel more at home in this country. The irony is that no, I do this for *my* sake. I do this for *my* sanity, for *my* peace of mind. I do this because it keeps *me* feeling whole and safe and alive; because it is who *I* am, who *I* have become. And I'll be the first to admit that I do this for very impractical reasons (despite the fact that there are also very real practical benefits) and ultimately for very selfish reasons: I am not willing to let go of the German language, the German culture. They are a part of me, intertwined together with my native English and my American language and culture. I don't want to have to decide, to choose, to have to sever ties with either of them. I want to belong to both and I want to pass on this duality to my children because, if anything, it is who I am and will always be.

Once my husband and I had decided that we would speak German at home with our children, we took on our task with gusto. No more unconscious wishy-washiness. We were now a German-speaking-household, and that was that. It felt firm, resolute and predictable and I felt a confidence and safety in our decision. When people asked, I had an answer. Our choice, however, threw my mother through an emotional loop of enormous proportions. She was in a state of shock when she first heard me speaking German with Patrick and even more so when Patrick started speaking his first words back to us, in German. She complained often that as a grandmother she couldn't even understand her first-born grandson's words. She was very upset, felt left out, and let us know. I presented her with a number of logical reasons, answered her concerns with research about the benefits of raising children bilingually and filled our discussion with published facts. But for both of us, this issue was above and beyond facts; this was an emotional issue upon which facts could not tread.

I often found myself answering my mother's questions with defensiveness. When she asked, "Will your children ever hear you say the words 'I love you'?" I answered "For goodness sakes, of course they will!" But would they? How did I know? How could I be so sure? And what might the consequences be if they never did? The truth is that at the time I didn't really think it mattered in which language they heard us say "I love you." I felt that all that mattered was that they heard us use such terms of endearment, regardless of language.

After a few months and with the help of a parenting group which my husband and I founded (the Bilingual/Bicultural Family Network), I came to realize that not only was my mother not unique in her concerns, but that there were many other families going through situations similar to ours. Through discussions with them, I was slowly reminded that with bilingualism, as with so many things in life, it was important to decide which battles were truly worth fighting. My mother and I arguing about language whenever we came together was unproductive and harmful to my family's bilingual efforts. And the most worrisome was the toll it was taking on the tenuous bond between us. In the end, we decided that it would be best for me to speak English when my mother was around and German when she wasn't, despite many warnings not to switch back and forth between languages. Amazingly enough, as time passed and our children got older, they fully embraced the "rules" of this arrangement. When their grandmother came to visit, they would tell me, "Mama, Grammy is coming to visit, so we'll be speaking English with you." As expected, after my mother left from an extended stay my children needed time to transition again back to as much German at home as before but ultimately they were willing participants and enjoyed their role as keepers of the "language rules."

Now that all three of my children have reached differing degrees of mastery over their languages, I find that I wonder how long I can maintain German as my home language. My vocabulary is not as plentiful and robust in German as it is in English and I sometimes fear that I may be holding back certain concepts from my children based on my limited ability to explain them. For the time being, I have been switching to English when I am unable to express something in German. I tell my children that I don't know all of the words in German for the topic and therefore will switch to English. As my children are still young, they accept this explanation at face value and assimilate it as simply another aspect of their bilingualism. Yet it still weighs heavily on my mind. Will there come a time when our discussions will only be in English? Should I spend a certain amount of time each day working on my German language skills in an effort to always be ahead of my children in their mastery of the language? To this I have no final answers. I will have to wait and see and follow my heart.

When I look back at who I was before I boarded that plane for Ireland, I ask myself whether it was all worth it. Was this thing called "international marriage" worth the emotional turmoil? Was it worth breaking with tradition and severing emotional ties with house and home? Some days I wonder what it would have been like to have stayed in my small town in California, to have married another American and to have raised monolingual children. There are moments when the simplicity of the image fills me with a bit of nostalgia for the way it was and what could have been. But when I look at my life today, I truly believe that taking the less trodden path was the right choice and that this decision has made all the difference. The only element I would have changed would have been my lack of confidence along the way; my lack of faith in the process. I still often second guess myself and my choices, concerned that I might be making the wrong decision, taking the wrong turn, unwittingly harming myself or others along the way. But at the very least, I savor the fact that I have been able to teach my children how to use the German past-tense, just in case they receive the wrong change back from a cashier while in Germany.

Mothering My Russian Speaking Kids
by Dee Thompson

In January 2003, the night before I met my daughter, I had an odd but very powerful dream. I was in an orphanage in a dark room. One figure, however, was bathed in light— an adorable little blonde girl. She walked up and looked at me, smiling, and raised her hands silently requesting that I pick her up. Somehow I knew that this child was mine. *I knew her.*

The dream didn't make much sense on Saturday morning when I first awoke, pinned beneath the scratchy wool blanket in the hotel room, listening to the snores of my roommate. I was part of a choir that traveled to Khabarovsk, in the Russian Far East, to sing Handel's Messiah with the local symphony.

The dream was still very vivid, but I couldn't fathom why I had dreamed it. Though I had always wanted a family, I had never before dreamed, literally, of having a child. I wasn't looking to adopt, either. I felt God was trying to tell me something, but that thought was rather scary.

At breakfast, we learned our evening concert had been canceled. One of our members, Danny Griffin, a musical missionary from Ohio, made a proposal to the group. Danny travels to Russia frequently and works closely with the children at Topolevo orphanage. He asked if we would be willing to go to the orphanage that night and sing for the children since our evening was unexpectedly free. All twenty of us agreed. Startled by the change of plans, especially the part about the orphanage, I couldn't stop thinking about the face of the child in my dream.

We arrived at the orphanage late that afternoon. It was a large, ramshackle building, very dark and forbidding. As we came to a stop, a little figure flew across the snow and waited for the bus doors to open. As they did, I stared down into the face of the child in my dream. An angelic-looking little doll with green eyes and short blonde, curly hair, she was wearing a grey and white striped sweater that was too big—but no coat despite the fact that the temperature was in the teens. I looked into her face in utter shock and I thought, *I know you!* But, of course, my rational mind said, *That's crazy.*

When I got off the bus I had to use the bathroom, and I asked Danny where it was located. Danny asked the tiny girl, in Russian, to show me to the bathroom. She took my hand and led me inside and down a dark hallway, then went up to a grown-up in an office and loudly and authoritatively asked for the key to a bathroom. She argued vehemently and I smiled to myself. *She has a lot of spirit!* I thought.

She then showed me to a locked bathroom with—joy of joys—a European potty. It was quite clean by Russian standards. She made a big effort for me and I was touched. When I came out, I gave her a piece of gum. I regretted that I didn't have anything else in my purse I thought she would like.

After we finished singing, the kids sang for us. Before we left, we passed out gifts, took photos, and hugged the children. Alesia, the little blonde girl, planted her arms around my neck and hugged tight to me, communicating, it seemed to me, *don't leave me, Mama.* I finally peeled off her arms and handed her off to another lady and ran back to the bus, where I sat inside and cried.

I had a deep and abiding sense that God showed her to me for a reason, that I was supposed to be her mom. Of course, my rational and logical mind rejected the idea, since I wasn't even thinking about adopting. However, I resolved to look into adopting her as soon as we got home.

When I got home and looked into adopting Alesia, it seemed such a daunting task that it was months before I even mentioned the idea to anyone. A few weeks after I got home I was stunned to learn, from a missionary who worked in the orphanage, that Alesia was eleven years old. Instant mom to an eleven-year-old who speaks no English?! Yikes.

I emailed an agency that worked in Khabarovsk and started to get an understanding of the many, many documents which would be required not just for the adoption, but for the homestudy. I spoke to a friend who was adopting domestically, and she advised me to raise money by getting a home equity line of credit on my house.

I wondered how Alesia and I would communicate. I worried how she would manage in school. I scoured the Internet trying to find resources, but there were very few. Most people adopt babies, not eleven-year-olds. I couldn't even find any memoirs about adopting an older child.

The adoption was delayed for many months. First, the orphanage director wouldn't even discuss an American adopting one of the orphans. After several months of prayer, and a letter from me (translated by my new friend, Kate

Humphrey, a young Russian woman who lives in my hometown), he relented and signed the authorization. Next, because Alesia wasn't listed on the database of Russian children available for adoption, we had to wait six more months to get her name entered and have her listed for the required time. During all that, I was gathering up documents for the homestudy and Russian dossier, and arranging for the home equity line.

In May of 2004 I was finally able to travel back to Khabarovsk for the first adoption trip. I had been sending Alesia letters for months, translated by Kate and delivered with the help of her aunt, who lives in Khabarovsk. Alesia felt she knew me, and I knew her. I visited with her for a few days, signed some papers, then had to return home. I was very sad when I got on the plane, but I was starting to see the end of the process.

I had other issues to contend with during those tumultuous months. I had to break off a romantic relationship because my boyfriend didn't want children. I started another relationship soon afterwards, but that one ended when he started seeing someone else. The company I worked for laid off a number of people, including me, but hired me back. Then they hired an attorney who didn't like me, and I had to quit and find another job.

Other factors made the adoption an incredible ordeal. Just traveling to Khabarovsk meant 20 hours of flights. I made the trip alone, twice. Once I started talking about adopting Alesia, a number of people told me I was crazy. They pointed out, rightly, that kids twelve or thirteen years old are difficult anyway, and such a child who spoke a different language and knew nothing of America would be incredibly difficult to manage. I thought about their words, and researched and planned, but the dire warnings didn't eradicate my deep feelings of purpose. They just made me more determined.

Finally, Alesia came home in December 2004, and life has never been the same.

From the moment I decided to adopt my daughter, her Russian heritage was a factor in our relationship. It's not a negative factor, just something I have to consider a lot. The first hurdle was language.

I have always thought communication is the most important thing in any relationship. I knew communicating with my daughter at first would be a challenge, so I decided to learn Russian.

I have a facility for languages. I studied French in high school and Italian in college and grad school. I love being able to communicate in a different language. Russian, however, proved to be far more difficult than I had imagined. I spent several weeks in a Russian language class before I admitted to really only wanting to learn "mommy" words. The instructor kindly gave me a list of those words, and even made a CD for me so I would learn correct pronunciation. I also listened to travel CDs in the car, and while working out. By the time I actually brought my daughter home, I knew enough words to stumble around in the language and learn the exact location of the nearest bus stop, and more importantly, to tell anyone who would listen to brush their teeth!

Once I got my daughter home, it immediately became clear that I was in way over my head. My chief form of communication with my daughter was by typing phrases into a website that did instant translations. Sometimes the translations were comical and puzzling. For instance, when I typed in "Do you like raw vegetables?" it was translated into "Do you like crude vegetables?" Sometimes, in desperation, I would call my friend Kate and get her to give Alesia important information in Russian.

Assimilating has been another challenge.

Because I had been to Russia, I should have known better, but I had the vague idea that from day one, my daughter would embrace All Things American, and transform herself instantly into the typical American child who was just a bit hampered by language. I couldn't imagine her not wanting to be completely American.

That magic transformation didn't happen, not surprisingly. She did come home from school the first day and ask me to get her a cell phone (I said nope). She watched American movies with enthusiasm. She also took to McDonald's immediately. However, she still wanted *pilmeni* (a Russian dumpling) and to hear Russian music and read Russian books. She delighted in meeting other kids who spoke Russian.

Once I finally caught on to the fact that my daughter wasn't going to instantly transform herself into a Typical American Kid, I began the process of trying to understand what it's like to grow up in the Russian culture, and more importantly, what it's like to be a Russian orphan. I knew I was going to have to meet her halfway, somehow.

I started doing even more research on the Internet, and joined groups of parents who had already adopted. I found out as much as I could about Russia, Russian orphans, and how to handle traumatized children.

Alesia spent six years in a Russian orphanage for older kids. Unlike the Desky Doms (babyhouses for babies and toddlers), the orphanages for older kids are usually rundown, depressing places. There was never enough food. There was only one set of clean clothes a week. There was little or no affection. Most possessions were stolen. The older kids routinely beat the younger ones. Alesia had learned to be tough and self-reliant to survive there.

Alesia was not terribly affectionate, at first. She was not used to it. Russians are not as affectionate as Americans, and she certainly didn't get affection in the orphanage. I didn't push it. She didn't want to give or receive hugs or kisses. I was unsure, too. With an adopted thirteen-year-old, what is appropriate? I had no one to ask. I gave her a kiss on the cheek when I tucked her into bed, and she usually kissed me on the cheek before heading to school. Then she went through a phase of giving me bear hugs, and laughing, when I kissed her goodnight before bed. We still struggle a bit with affection, with knowing what's best for each of us. She has asked me, with exasperation at times, "Why is it so important to hug?!" My lame answer about hugs releasing endorphins was met with a look of suspicion.

Another huge adjustment was to get Alesia used to dressing modestly. In Russia, most young women dress very provocatively. Tight pants, low cut blouses, short skirts—all are perfectly normal and accepted in Russian society. Had I not been really strict with her, Alesia would have preferred to dress like that. That's what she was used to seeing. Young

Russian women are still often taught that it's very important to dress in order to get a man—a 1950's sort of mentality that started in the 1940's when so many young men were killed in World War II, and persists to this day. Alesia was told in the orphanage that she was so pretty, she would be able to find a man in America, and he would take care of her, as all Americans are rich.

Every behavioral issue I encounter causes me to have to ponder it from many different angles. Is it just a kid thing, or a Russian thing? Is it an orphanage behavior? Sometimes it's just an Alesia behavior. For instance, she can be bossy. I think that crosses all cultural boundaries. Trying to teach her to drop that natural bossiness and be more obedient, gracious and well mannered is tough, but we live in the South. Children in my family are expected to behave, and I am strict about that. Also, my mother lives with us. Just getting Alesia to say "ma'am" and "sir" was a chore, until I had my friend Kate, who is Russian, explain that it's simply a way of being respectful.

I recently started taking Alesia to a therapist, a woman from the country of Georgia who speaks Russian and has worked a lot with adopted children. She has helped Alesia to understand that some of her difficulties in relationships and at school are due to trauma she suffered in early life. She has also helped me to understand Alesia and our relationship is much better. I also have a better understanding of how Russians view orphans and how this impacted Alesia. Children are rarely taken away from birthparents, for instance, unless their lives are in danger.

Last year, I adopted a little boy from Kazakhstan. I wanted Alesia to have a sibling, and I felt a little boy would be the best match. I also decided to adopt a Russian speaking child, so Alesia would better bond with him. From the moment he came to America, Alesia has embraced Michael and she cares for him, teaches him, plays with him, and is generally a wonderful big sister.

Michael has adapted quickly and easily to being an American boy. Amazingly, he doesn't even remember how to speak Russian. He likes *pilmeni* and will sometimes fondly recall Russian foods, but he has assimilated much more readily and easily than my daughter. Even his accent is almost gone.

Alesia has never totally shed her Russian accent, and likely won't, without a lot of help. We live in Atlanta, so people notice right away. When people ask where she is from, she usually just says "I came from Russia," and offers no more information.

We talk about how Alesia feels about her heritage. I have explained that her birthmother wasn't a bad person; she simply couldn't take care of Alesia. I even showed her the court papers about the relinquishment hearing, shortly after she came home. She had been holding onto a fantasy that her birthmom didn't know where she was because she was removed from her home and put in a hospital far away. I thought it was important for her to know that was not true. Alesia wants to go back to Russia one day and find her birthmother and I will support that. She needs to understand what happened and why. So many Russian kids go to orphanages because their parents are just poor, but often they are also, like Alesia's birthmom, alcoholics.

Straddling two cultures has been a big challenge for my daughter. All kids ask questions about their identities when they are teens, and Alesia has said a few times when she was stressed "Why did you even adopt me?" (My answer is always the same—because God told me you were my daughter, and I wanted a daughter.)

Alesia has made great progress in feeling good about herself. When I went to my first parent teacher conference at her school, in 8th grade, all the teachers were astonished I spoke English so well. I had to explain that Alesia was adopted. She had not wanted to tell them.

At the end of her freshman year in high school, her ESL English teacher asked each student to take photos of their homes and families that document their ethnicity. Their ethnography project was a way to understand and celebrate their cultural heritages. It was assumed that all the students came from non-English speaking homes.

I helped Alesia with the project. She didn't want to do it, because it confused her, and I think it somehow scared her. She had to give a presentation to the class about the fact that her heritage is both Russian and American. I helped her take the photos. We photographed her collection of Russian dolls, my collection of icons, and some Russian foods we buy routinely. I photographed both kids holding their passports, which are not American. Alesia had to arrange the photos and write captions. I proofread the captions but didn't make many changes.

In the end, Alesia did well on her ethnography project,

and made it her own. She was able to stand in front of her entire class, which included several Russian kids from Russian families, and explain to them about her dual heritage. She was able to say, without embarrassment, that her life will always include two cultures, Russian and American.

When I was getting ready to adopt my son, I asked Alesia to help me with a small book I was writing for him in both Russian and English. I wanted him to understand how different it is to live in a family and in America. I called it "Jack's New Family." Alesia gave suggestions and validated all the information about how it feels to come to a new country, with a new mom, and how strange it is to try to fit in. It was a labor of love, to help her little brother.

In the front of the book, this is my dedication: To my children, whose love and courage inspire me every day.

I take pride in the fact that my family is unique. I teach my children that diversity is good, and that they should be proud of their birth countries. We watch movies about Russia and Kazakhstan. We speak Russian sometimes. I have friends who are Russian. The kids have friends who are Russian, Kazakh, and Ukrainian.

The most important thing I try to teach my kids is this: Our family comes from here, Russia, and Kazakhstan, but we are all American, and we were put together by love.

Care and Feeding
by Kate MacVean

¿No te gusta el cordero? You don't like lamb? Every
summer the same question from my husband's uncle. The
region in Spain where my mother-in-law grew up was full of
shepherds, and even now that the livestock and bustling
village life have given way to cars and summer homes, roast
lamb is still the dish of choice during the *fiestas*. Her brother
smiles when he asks, and I don't know if it is just to make
conversation, or if it bothers him, child of the lean years after
the Spanish Civil War, that I afford myself the luxury of not
liking such a succulent dish. When he and my mother-in-
law, Feli, were growing up, their diets consisted mainly of
garbanzos, fatback, and potatoes, with the occasional dairy
product thrown in when available. More than half a century
later, they can afford to eat what they want, but the memories must remain. I return the smile and say that the lamb
smells good, but just doesn't agree with me.

Back home in the States I did not consider myself a
picky eater, but here, it appears, I am. Though I had left my
flirtations with vegetarianism behind me, in the early
months after coming here I would argue with my husband
Santi over the optimal amount and frequency of meat
consumption for our then still-hypothetical children. But
then I became accustomed to the leg of cured ham with hoof
still attached, perched in its stand on our kitchen counter,

and even became partial to the long strips of this delicacy that Santi sliced off with a long, flat knife. I acquired a taste for squid and relished slices of octopus, complete with suction-cup tentacle, sautéed with garlic and paprika, and even added beef back into my diet once and for all.

Even so, for the most part I still prefer my meat skinless, boneless, and preferably curried or stir-fried; in short, as far removed from its animal origin as possible. The Spanish, however, are a meat-loving people, and dig in with gusto, undeterred by gristle, fat, and tendons. The lamb roast is heavy on all of these and greasy to boot, so at these summer meals, I fill up on the first course and make my excuses.

Feli is used to this, and makes no comment, but I know she is hoping I don't pass my finicky ways down to my kids, her grandchildren. It's true, life is much easier for people like my husband who eat anything without issue, and it would be nice if our kids took after him in this regard. So I enjoy watching Elías, 4, tuck into a *tapa* of bread topped with blood sausage, and can't help but cringe when Pedro, 6, nibbles at his slices of *lomo adobado*, pork loin seasoned with garlic and paprika, leaving the rinds in neat piles off to the side. Like me, he is meticulous about separating the tiny bones from his fish, and often tries to remove the skin as well. Is it genetic, or has he picked this up from me, despite my half-hearted attempts at dissimulation?

What seems an unfortunate quirk to me is something potentially more serious to my mother-in-law. Though I was familiar with the stereotype of the Old World Italian grandmother, chasing her progeny around the table with plates of food, exhorting them to "Eat! Eat!" I was not prepared for this Spanish version. Feli hovers over the kids at mealtimes, registering every bite. She frets over their tall, lean bodies, despite my reassurances that they are not starving. After a good meal, she beams: "Seeing them eat, it's as if I have already eaten myself!" If they don't eat enough, she brings it up hours later, mouth drawn with worry.

I read books and parenting magazines from the States, which confirm my more laid-back approach: "Offer your child a variety of healthy foods, but don't worry if their intake on any particular day is imbalanced. Chances are it will all even out over the course of the week." "Don't let the dinner table turn into a power struggle."

Even the photocopied instruction sheet from our Spanish pediatrician warns: "Mealtimes should be relaxed. Never force a child to clean his plate."

But Feli operates under her own set of rules, in which a mother's most important job is to make sure her children are well-nourished: the right foods in the right amounts at every meal. Though she is careful not to criticize me directly, she berates my husband for not eating enough fruit, legumes, and vegetables, or for not having breakfast before he leaves for work. She reads aloud from her healthy living magazines: "Listen to all the nutritional properties there are in an artichoke!" or "Here's a recipe for how to make a supervitamin drink for times of stress!" Most of the time she lives with her other son, several hours away, and when she is visiting us she phones him to ask what he has eaten that day, suffering because she is not there to cook.

Here, too, she swoops in and takes over the daily shopping and cooking, whipping up a *cocido*, garbanzo stew, for lunch, and breaded fish with zucchini soup for dinner. Feli has been coming for extended visits since before Pedro was born, to lend a hand while I've been pregnant, or trying to study for exams with the kids underfoot, or going out of my mind on hot summer days waiting for school to finally start again. I am grateful for her help with the kids and her skill in the kitchen, but it comes at a price: when she is here, the anxiety level in the house gets ratcheted up substantially, especially when she supervises the kids' meals.

Like a commanding officer, she stands over her reluctant troops with a fresh round of ammunition always at hand: "Quick! Let's see who can finish first!" "If you eat it all, I'll give you a surprise!" "If you don't eat it, you won't grow—you'll just stay little!" "If you don't eat it, no surprise for you!"

"Make him finish," she admonishes me. "You feed it to him; otherwise he won't eat it." Battle-weary, I find myself spooning soup into the mouth of my four-year-old, who has been feeding himself since he was 12 months. Pleased by the extra attention, he opens wide for each bite. Finally, lunch is over.

When 5 pm rolls around, it's time for the *merienda*, afternoon snack: she slices white bread from the bakery, toasts it, and drizzles it with olive oil. With a pair of scissors, she cuts the slices of cured ham into manageable bites for the filling. Finally, she pulls several oranges out of the drawer and squeezes them for juice.

It's a good snack, and the kids appreciate it—sometimes. Other days, they complain, "Oh no, not ham again!"

or just aren't hungry. On those days, Feli worries, and tells me over and over again, "I always gave my boys a sandwich after school. The doctors say they need to eat a sandwich to keep their energy up."

A couple of weeks later her visit is over, and mealtimes are once again relatively calm. But it doesn't take long for the needling to start in, this time from me. "Just eat it, Pedro! You like everything in it!" It's pasta with zucchini, red bell pepper, walnut, and cheese. He does like everything in it, though for some reason he insists he only wants to eat the pasta, not the zucchini, and the cheese is too melty, and why can't we just pour tomato sauce over it? It's not until I stoop to a tactic I despise, threat of punishment, that I see results: "Eat it or no TV after lunch," I snap, and he eats it all without comment. Then Elías jumps into the fray, eating all of the pasta but piling his veggies on the table and refusing, with the vehemence of the four-year-old that he is, to touch them. Knowing he doesn't like red pepper, I tell him he can choose to eat either the one piece of pepper or the three small pieces of zucchini. Surprisingly, he chooses the pepper, and chews it for a minute before spitting it into his bowl. "Well, I guess you can try the zucchini instead," I tell him, but he answers, "No, I kind of liked it," and retrieves the pepper and pops it back into his mouth.

Other times, things go less smoothly, and I wonder, where did I go wrong? When I take a more laissez-faire approach, Pedro divides his already small serving of meat into two on the plate, announcing that he will only eat half. Elías, left to his own devices, eschews the vegetables he often likes but is now not in the mood for. Both of them pick at their food, complaining, acting like it is wholly unreasonable to expect them to eat one bowl of lentils, which they have happily consumed countless other times in the past. Why does it so often seem like mealtimes will drag on for hours, as they lift the paella on their forks, one grain of rice at a time, protesting "I'm not hungry," only to reappear in the kitchen half an hour later looking for a snack?

This is normal kid behavior, or so I'm told, but I can't help wondering. If they hadn't been exposed to so much mealtime drama from their grandmother, would we be having these problems now? Free from undue pressure, would they have settled into a routine of calmly eating until they were full, not averse to trying new combinations once in awhile? Would food have become a genuine non-issue, *a la* Penelope Leach?

There's no way to know. I take comfort from the fact that they are both still young, with plenty of time to grow into new habits. I suspect that Pedro will always share my aversion to certain kinds of meat, but he is slowly becoming more willing to try new foods. Elías can be quite adventuresome, when he's not being stubborn, and even drank down a whole glass of vegetable stock, bitter with greens, that I had left on the counter while cooking just the other day.

My burden of worry is lighter than Feli's: I know they will be fine. The only real risk is that they may miss out on new experiences or be thought finicky or rude for not eating certain things. I am lucky that Santi's family looks past my refusal of their feast, just as I am lucky that we can afford to feed our own family such a rich selection of foods and never for a minute worry about starvation or malnutrition. While the constant badgering about food is wearing, I know it comes from the right place. In the end, there is no need to worry about the boys: both of them are strong and healthy, and loved.

So Are You American or Malaysian?
by Juli Herman

"I'm Asian-American," declares my eight-year-old as he clears up the table while I tend to a pot on the stove.

I remain silent and wait for more. Chatty by nature, he never fails to churn out interesting conversation to keep me entertained in the kitchen. After that first statement, I'm sure there's more to come. Sure enough, he continues,

"*Abi* said Asian-Americans are very rare."

An image of a new rare animal species pops in my head, and I stifle the urge to chuckle. What has dear husband been telling his son?

"Rare? There're so many Asian-Americans. Japanese, Koreans, Chinese…" I respond.

He looks up, his glasses sliding down the bridge of his nose. "Oh…I think he said *Malaysian*-American! Yeah! Malaysian-American. There're not many Malaysian-Americans."

He says it with some finality, as if putting an end to all rebuttals. He tilts his face slightly upwards to stop his glasses from sliding further down his nose. His expression is so serious that I feel a guffaw making its way up my throat.

Leave it to my eight-year-old to give me some food for thought. I had never thought of my children as Malaysian-Americans. Well, at least I have never termed it as such. To me, they're both Americans and Malaysians, but not

Malaysian-Americans.

When asked, "So are you American or Malaysian?" They would respond with their own individual answers, in the context of what they think being Malaysian is about.

From my son: "I'm both, because Abi said so." Again, we see the influence of dear husband on impressionable dear son.

From my middle child: "I'm American because I don't like spicy Malaysian food, and I don't like rice very much."

From my firstborn, now eleven: "I'm Malayrican, because you're from Malaysia and we're in America."

At other times, we would get the guilt-inducing answer, "No, because I don't do much Malay stuff, and don't speak Malay that much."

And that brings to mind the question: isn't it the parents' responsibility to make sure their native tongue stays intact in their offspring? We always thought we would return to Malaysia a few years after we both graduated from Iowa State. It never occurred to us to immerse the children in our native tongue while we were still in the United States. We took solace in the well-known fact that children pick up new languages easily, so we focused on immersing them in English instead, in order to get the best of both worlds.

Eleven years later, we are still in the United States. Our firstborn is now eleven, and even though she understands Malay, she doesn't speak it. I very rarely, if ever, spoke English to her in her infancy. Malay was the main language we used with her for the first two years of her life. That was, until someone asked her a question in English, to which she responded with silence. Woe to us! Our daughter didn't understand English!

We began to speak English in the house, at least with her. Two additional children later, English had become the main spoken language in our home. Malay was only for the parents. Child number two and three never received much Malay in their infancies. We realized later on that our daughter's silence was due to shyness, not lack of comprehension, but by then, English had established its roots as the communication medium between us and our children.

People would say to us, "They can easily pick up Malay when you all return to Malaysia."

A few years later though, the remarks had turned to, "You don't speak your language with them?"

"They'll have trouble making friends back home, because the other kids might make fun of them for not speaking the language."

The latter remark struck me deeply. Initially, I was annoyed. These remarks only ruffled my feathers, and made me dig my heels in deeper. But imagining my children being ridiculed, the maternal part of me mollified the annoyance and I admitted to the mistake on our part. Now, when people ask me, "You don't speak your language with them?" I reply, "No. We made a mistake. We should have."

This is not to say that they haven't been exposed to our native tongue at all. When anger consumes me and rationale abandons me, along with any translating abilities I might have, I often resort to spewing out Malay phrases in furious bursts.

Other than that unplanned exposure, they also know the Malay words for 'sleep', 'pee', and 'poop'. In fact, for several blissful years, knowing these words in Malay has been to our advantage, as we could easily ask if they wanted to pee or poop in Malay without being discreet in public. That was until we went back to Malaysia for a visit. To my chagrin, I found myself asking my daughter out loud, out of habit, in a parking lot, within earshot of Malay-speaking people, "Do you need to go poop?" Let's just say there are less embarrassing ways of asking your child if she needs to go to the bathroom in Malay than the crude version I was using.

In an attempt to introduce our native tongue to our children, my husband started to consciously speak more Malay to them. I, on the other hand, gave up trying because it was much easier to go through the day without having to explain every word I was saying. However, my husband's effort didn't go unrewarded. In the beginning, they responded with blank stares and cocked heads. But he persisted. Before long, their natural curiosity took over, and we began to hear, "*Makan*" being called out instead of "Eat!"

We were getting somewhere, though I couldn't stop myself from chuckling at their American-accented Malay.

It was not all bad when they understood less Malay, for my husband and I were able to have conversations that were not meant for little ears to hear. Nevertheless, since our oldest had been immersed in the language for the first two years of her life, our secret conversations were not completely secret, and to this day, she understands more Malay than her siblings.

Fortunately for us, both sets of grandparents speak and understand English, though from the children's perspective, it may not seem so.

"I can't understand what Atok's saying," complains my daughter as she hands me the phone receiver, leaving me with the task of explaining to my father that his granddaughter does not understand his spoken English.

"And he keeps asking what I was saying," she adds.

It goes both ways it seems. Our children have trouble understanding their grandparents' Malay accent in their spoken English, and their grandparents have trouble understanding their grandchildren's American accent.

If the children have any Malay in them, it would probably be in their taste buds. Even though my culinary skills do not always produce authentic Malaysian dishes, I have managed to put Malaysian cuisine on our table throughout the years. Our meals usually consist of rice or noodles, stir-fried vegetables, and a meat or chicken dish.

Since Malaysian cuisine is a blend of Malay, Indian and Chinese cuisines, with some Arab and Portuguese influences, our food has a wide range of tastes: salty, creamy, spicy, tangy, sour, and sweet. Spicy is my biggest hurdle when it comes to cooking for the family.

Since my husband and I weren't willing to give up our love for hot and spicy food, when our oldest daughter graduated from baby food to adult food, I trained her to tolerate hot dishes by always having a glass of whole milk nearby. When the familiar symptoms appear, which included frantic hisses, watery eyes, and sometimes flailing hands, we would hand her a glass of cold milk. The casein in milk has proven again and again to do its wonderful job of surrounding the offending capsaicin molecules from the chili peppers, and sloshing them uneventfully down her throat.

I was determined not to have to cook two separate meals in our household as my stepmother had done due to my younger brothers' intolerance to spicy food. My firstborn thus grew up eating spicy food, much to my delight and relief. Alas! My second-born hates it with a gusto.

"Why does everything have to be so spicy?"

"I hate meanie spicy food!"

This is the child who claims she's American because she doesn't like hot Malaysian food. Her younger brother, on the other hand, seems to have inherited my Malaysian taste buds, and adores Malaysian food, spicy or not. He would happily eat bean sprouts stir-fried with soy sauce and bird's eye chili.

Even though most traditional Malay dishes are spicy, there are quite a number of mild ones for those who can't tolerate the endorphin-releasing burn associated with chili peppers. And this is where my nine year-old shows her appreciation for Malaysian food.

"*Ummi*, what's the name of this?" she asked, referring to a chicken dish braised in an infusion of coriander, cumin, cloves, cardamom, cinnamon, and coconut milk.

"*Korma Ayam*," I replied.

"It's delicious!" she exclaimed, beaming with joy.

There was a time when I wouldn't bother telling them the Malay name of the dishes I made, for the same reason I quit trying to speak Malay to them. Years and several loved Malaysian food items later though, it became a problem.

"*Ummi*, can you make that green thingy-a-bomb?"

Green is the color of most Malaysian desserts, as we love to use the fragrant leaves of the *pandan* tree to flavor our sweets. "Green thingy-a-bomb" does nothing to narrow it down to a specific dessert. That's when I decided to introduce them to the Malay name of anything Malaysian I make, and that's also when they decided they had better know the Malay name of any Malaysian food they like, so they could demand it without having to play Twenty Questions.

One food item they all love and know by its Malay name is *Nasi Lemak,* a popular breakfast item in Malaysia, which also happens to be one of my favorite Malaysian dishes.

One morning, I was driving home with my oldest daughter from the tennis court. Struck by nostalgia, I suddenly had a craving for the aromatic rice cooked in coconut milk and eaten with a spicy accompaniment called *sambal,* a few wedges of boiled eggs, and fresh cucumber slices. With the intent of sharing my Malaysian experience with my American-born and raised daughter, I said,

"In Malaysia, on mornings like this, there are stalls on the sides of the street selling *Nasi Lemak.* They would wrap it in banana leaves, and when you open it, ahh the fragrance!"

"That sounds like olden times," she responded.

Understandably, having lived most of her life in Ames, Iowa, and Columbus, Ohio, she couldn't imagine such a setting. At that moment, I felt sorry for my children, for not having had the opportunity to witness and experience the bustling city life of Kuala Lumpur that is rich with a variety of cultural adventures.

With a combination of reminiscence and chronic craving, I would at times tell my children of the fruits I enjoyed devouring growing up. When I talk of the hairy red fruits called rambutan, or the spiky, thorny, and controversial-smelling fruit called durian, they either screw up their faces in disgust or giggle at the descriptions.

The closest we could get to a rambutan in the States is to buy the canned, peeled and pitted version at Asian grocery stores. However, my children abhor going to Asian groceries. As soon as they realize our destination, groans erupt from the back of the van.

"It's stinky!"

"Argh! Why do we have to go there?"

Nevertheless, these trips are a must, since that's where we get the bulk of ingredients to keep the taste of Malaysia in our kitchen. Every now and then, when cravings strike me, I grab cans of rambutan, lychees, and longans at the Asian grocery store.

At home, while I slowly savor my canned Malaysian fruits, they approach me with curiosity.

"What's that?"

"Here, you wanna taste some? Try it," I say, offering them a longan or two.

Sometimes they let me pop one in their mouths. Sometimes, they recoil and back away. Recently, my oldest daughter's curiosity overcame her fear and disgust. With some trepidation, she allowed me to feed her one. Immediately loving it, she now jumps up excitedly whenever I open my can of longans. In fact, she even asks me if she could open one for herself. No longer can I hog those costly cans to myself. Until we return to Malaysia or go there for a visit during its various fruit seasons, we'll just have to make do with the canned versions.

Nevertheless, my children's taste buds are apparently more diverse than mine, since they are also exposed to the American style of eating. When my mother came to visit us a year ago, she grimaced when she saw them slathering peanut butter on cut apple slices.

"How can you eat apple with peanut butter?!"

"But it's really good, Grandma!" they insisted.

My mother responded with a rapid shake of the head and a disgusted expression. I remember chuckling at the incident. Yet, I also share my mother's sentiments. I would turn up my nose at the idea of eating a celery stick spread with peanut butter, and I never understood how they could tolerate the combination of sweet juicy apple with the creaminess of peanut butter.

Despite the obvious signs, I was oblivious to the realization that my children will never become one hundred percent Malaysians, until recently. By three separate self proclamations, I now have a Malayrican, an American, and a Malaysian American loving and hating Malaysian food, while rendering the Malay language to 'Malaysian-American speak'. I wonder what the toddler will proclaim himself to be when he can express his opinion on the matter. But for now, I think I will enjoy cringing and chuckling at their attempts to speak Malay, bore them with hairy and thorny descriptions of exotic tropical fruits of Southeast Asia, and maybe try to hide the cans of longans from my fellow longan lover.

Some Olympic Wisdom for My Home Team
by Rose Kent

"Check this out, Mom! One of ours is catching up!" my son Connor shouts as I walk into the family room with a bowl of popcorn. He is pointing at the television and pumping his fist in the air. It is a hot and sticky summer night in upstate New York, and my family is sprawled across the couch, cheering as the world's top athletes go for gold at the Olympics in Beijing.

I look at the TV. Runners zoom around the track on turbo-charged sneakers for the 1,500-meter race. I can't help but state the obvious. These guys are fast! A wiry Kenyan leads the pack, followed by a long-legged Russian with a tattoo on his shoulder. A small Ethiopian runner is right at the Russian's heels, a gold chain bouncing against his chest. Skin tones range from pasty pale to rich deep chocolate.

As the men jockey to capture the lead I search for the USA runner that Connor is excited about, but the only American I see has fallen behind.

"Which one?" I ask Connor.

He points to a lanky man with red bushy hair, his arms pumping as he attempts to break away from the pack. "Ireland" is printed on the back of his jersey.

"C'mon Irish dude. Smoke these guys!" Connor cheers,

his plump face lit up like the Olympic torch.

I smile. Oh, okay. I get it now. The Irish runner.

One glance at Connor's face might make this comment seem bizarre. The Irish runner is one of ours? Obviously Connor doesn't hail from Dublin. Connor is South Korean by birth and American by adoption. Thirteen years ago he arrived at JFK Airport in New York at the wee age of four months, direct from Pusan, a port city in southeastern South Korea. We gave him the nickname Buddha Baby and fittingly so, given his moon belly, apple cheeks, and bright laughing eyes.

Like other parents with children born in other countries, I paid attention during adoptive parenting training sessions. Agency social workers made the point very clearly: Culture matters. Don't raise your son like a vanilla child with your heritage. Adoptees need to learn about their native culture so they can develop a full sense of ethnic identity. It's your job, adoptive parent, to make this happen, even if it takes extra effort to do so in homogenized suburban America. Twenty years ago this wasn't the case. A just-treat-them-like-they're-white style of adoptive parenting was practiced, and it resulted in some Korean kids who grew into Korean adults who felt out of place with other Asians and confused about their identity.

Of course, learning about being a multiracial family wasn't completely new for me. Our family has never been all white. Connor's adoptive father, Tae, was born in Korea, the son of a Korean woman from a remote village and an American GI who was part black and part Cherokee Indian.

Tae was born in that same village. Minutes after he arrived the village medicine man performed a traditional dance and assigned him his name. People traveled for miles, curious to get a peek at this "large, dark, half-American baby." (He weighed ten pounds.)

With red hair, freckles and a pronounced stubborn streak, I bring Irish looks and ancestry to my family. Three of my four grandparents came from farms on the Emerald Isle, arriving in New York City shortly after the Depression, young and poor, but determined to find The Great American Dream that they'd heard about on the other side of the Atlantic. Nearly one hundred years later, their hopefulness still inspires me, and I've often shared their stories of struggle and triumph with Connor and his three siblings.

Tae junior and Kellyrose, my birth children now in their twenties, are part black, part Korean, part American Indian, and part white. (Or, as Kelly used to say as a little girl when she introduced herself, "I've got lots of good stuff mixed inside of me.") And while Connor and his younger sister, Theresa, are both Korean and adopted, they are not biological siblings. Connor comes from Pusan; and Theresa, from Taegue, two separate and distinct cities in Korea. They couldn't have more different personalities, looks, and body shapes. All of my four children, then, have grown up with siblings and parents who don't look quite like them. Being different is the norm in my house, as familiar as piled-high laundry and bags of snacks on the kitchen counter.

That's not to say I considered the job of educating my adopted kids on their native culture a given, simply because our family had some Korean roots. I live in sprawling suburbia with a McDonald's and a mall every twenty miles. The schools are majority white, and I'm as vulnerable as the next mom to sticking with a lifestyle that doesn't look outside the American box, so to speak. So from early on, I made it a mission to bring culture inside our home. We served Korean food like *mandu* and *bulgogi*. (Lucky me; these dishes are delicious.) We got to know Koreans in our community. We celebrated Korean holidays like *Chuesok* (Thanksgiving) and *Seol-nal* (Lunar New Year). We ate with chopsticks (The kids and their dad took to this well. I am still hopelessly clumsy.) We hung Korean flags in Connor's and Theresa's bedrooms, and we decorated our home with beautiful Asian tapestries and celadon pottery. All four children attended Camp MuJiGae, a wonderful summer cultural camp for Korean adopted kids.

At times I went overboard teaching Korean Culture 101. You know, Korean food too many nights in a row when my kids craved pizza. There was the year I drove two hundred miles so Connor and Theresa could attend a Christmas party for Korean adoption children. For four hours they ran wild playing Korean games in a hot auditorium with a hundred adopted kids until a tired and cranky Connor declared, "I wanna go home! I'm tired of all this Korean stuff!" And sometimes I discussed sensitive adoption topics with the kids before they were able to handle them.

Underneath my blundering efforts was a nagging fear. What if my attempt to educate them on culture wasn't enough? What if Connor and Theresa suffered pain and sadness over their adoption? What if I didn't protect them? I shared this once with a wise adult adoptee who looked at me like I was clueless. 'You can't take away the pain that accompanies adoption," she said. "It's their grief and they have a right to it." The best I could do, she said, was to love them and be there to help them learn and grow in many aspects of their lives.

Hearing that seemingly simple advice was eye opening. I lightened up. It also influenced my professional life. For years I had been a business writer, but I turned to fiction and published my first children's novel, *Kimchi & Calamari* (HarperCollins Publishers). Surprise, it's the tale about a wisecracking adopted Korean boy living in a blue-collar Italian family, who gets himself into an awkward middle school dilemma that eventually leads him to search for his birth mother.

Something else happened on the path to keeping my Korean kids connected to Korea. Connor developed a strong sense of pride about his family heritage, or "all that good stuff mixed inside our family," as Kelly might say. I get zippo credit for this. I should have expected (and encouraged) this interconnected sense of family heritage, but I didn't. I was too busy worrying about the kids' individual identities. It's true that we parents don't always see the forest for the trees. (Sometimes I don't even see that we're out of detergent.)

Connor became the one to remind his parents and his brothers and sisters to wear green on Saint Patrick's Day and for me, to prepare his favorite dinner, Irish shepherd's pie. The bedtime story that best comforted him was the one explaining how he was named after two strong brave Irishmen: my godfather, Mike Connor, a strapping (and kind-hearted) six foot Irishman from County Cork who, like

Connor, fell in love with American sports; and Conor Larken, the brave Irish rebel in Leon Uris' epic novel *Trinity*. Connor has developed an appreciation for the history of Ireland and its people. And I've also shared with him how Koreans have been called "The Irish of Asia" because, like the Irish, Koreans are known for their determination and stubborn spirit after a long history of being invaded and oppressed.

So Connor's ethnic pride includes his natural Koreanness, his mom's Irishness, and more. He takes special satisfaction in hearing about the accomplishments of African-American achievers because he feels related to them, too, through his siblings' black heritage, and he knows the complicated role that race still plays in our country. And I can still recall the day he came home from fourth grade upset about learning the real deal about America's Native Americans. "We're related to them, and they sure got jerked around," he told me, shaking his head.

It's the final lap now of the 1,500-meter race, and the Irish runner has run out of gas and dropped back. It's come down to a three-man sneaker slugfest between two Kenyans and the Ethiopian runner. We're all on our feet now, shouting and whistling, and Connor has a huge smile on his face when the smaller Kenyan crosses the finish line first to win the gold medal. "Way to go Kenya!" he shouts, prideful like we can claim this one, too.

Global cheering not withstanding, I don't worry that Connor lacks patriotism. American athletes hold a special place in his sports-crazy heart. Like many of his friends, he raved about Michael Phelps, the all-American swimmer who took home a record eight gold medals. And he high-fived his brother when the men's basketball team slam-dunked their way to the gold too, since that's the sport he plays. Still, I couldn't hide my delight when Connor glowed just as brightly when the South Korean baseball team upset the heavily favored Cubans in the baseball finals. And again, when Jamaican sprinter Usain Bolt shattered the world record in the 100-meter race, Connor took a lap around our family room, mimicking Bolt's body language and shouting, "We did it again!" (Technically nobody in our family is Jamaican, but I didn't have the heart to tell him.)

Appreciating Korean culture has been a whole different story for Theresa, my Air Aeropostale-wearing, Disney-wannabe daughter. She's not very interested in Korean food or history, never mind Irish stories and the rest of the ethnic jazz her mom keeps talking up. And when it comes to the Olympics, the track and field and swim races don't captivate her nearly as much as women's gymnastics. But the Chinese gymnasts do not impress her, no matter that I point out their success, or that they have taut petite bodies like hers. She doesn't get excited when she learns that the women's gold medal on vault goes to a girl from North Korea. What best delights her? Those blonde pony tailed Team USA gymnasts wearing shiny red, white and blue bodysuits. These are her idols, the ones she pretends to be when she does cartwheels in the backyard.

Is this healthy? Have I done something wrong? The voices of adoptive social workers echo in my head. Culture matters. I can't help but worry when my Asian daughter aspires to look and act like what's she's not—and shouldn't be. Why is Theresa more drawn to white Disney sitcom stars than anything related to Korea? I feel like this battle against pop culture is all uphill, but I want to fight it for her. You see, I've heard of that ugly slur "Twinkie," describing Asians as yellow on the outside and white on the inside. I don't want that thrown at her.

Weeks later, the Beijing Olympics are history. American gold medalists return to fat endorsement contracts and their images on cereal boxes and commercials. My kids head back to school, and on the first day, they are each given an assignment.

Connor must write a personal narrative introducing himself to his teachers. When he's finished, he asks me to check it over, and I do. In the first paragraph he shares that he is unique because of his Korean birth and his "special blended family." And I'm not the least bit shocked when I read about how much he loves playing sports and watching Olympic athletes from all over the globe.

I look at Theresa's homework next. Her assignment was to decorate a writing journal with pictures, words and drawings reflecting who she is.

But now the surprise is on me, because right there in the center of the page—between the wrapper of her favorite gum and the face of a blonde Disney star—is a large picture of the Korean flag. The red and blue taegeuk with the black parallel lines in each corner.

So she does get it, I think. In her own way, she is Korean and proud.

Now that to me feels like Olympic gold.

Promises to Myself
by Devorah Lifshutz

It's 1967 and I'm seven years old, having dinner with my parents at our home in New York. My mother is ladling out chicken soup and speaking, almost yelling, to my father in Hungarian.

"Speak English," I yell. I can't understand anything they are saying and they know it's their fault. They are the ones who refused to teach me Hungarian.

My parents look at me sadly and then at each other.

"See, we're speaking English now," my father says smiling at me apologetically as he brings a spoonful of soup to his mouth.

"Ah, he says, rolling his head back contentedly. " This is like medicine."

I smirk. I know it's a compliment, some old country phrase that doesn't translate, but it sounds funny to me, like my mother is feeding us Robitussin or Triaminic expectorant.

After that, my parents slip back into Hungarian, hardly conscious that they've made the switch. It is their mother tongue after all, even if mother had been a toxic parent.

My parents are Hungarian Jews, survivors. I am their only daughter, born a decade and a half after the war. My parents want me to be an American, a real Yankee Doodle, even if that carries me away from them.

At bedtime, my parents never tell stories of the past, not even pleasant tales of holidays or apple picking or swimming in cool rivers and they certainly don't talk about the camps they were in. Instead, my mother sits on my red brocaded bedspread reading to me Madeline and Curious George and Dr. Seuss in her heavily accented English.

My favorite game is pretending, creating elaborate scenarios involving a different family with different parents, parents who are young and slim, who speak without accents, who play tennis and barbecue burgers and franks and weren't in "the war."

When I have my own family I promise myself that is how it will be.

Years later, I learn that parents are meant to be role models, templates for their children to copy, models for life. I can't imagine copying my parents. They seem so distant, so foreign, so odd, and yet at the same time almost superhuman when I consider the suffering they experienced.

When I'm twenty five I leave the US and move to Israel, not as an immigrant. I'm no die hard Zionist, but I'm an old maid—twenty five is old in orthodox Jewish circles—and Jerusalem has a large, untapped supply of eligible American Jewish men. I promise myself that I will get married, raise a family, with lots of kids to replace the family Hitler destroyed.

I'm hopeful that in this new country my luck will change. This is the Holy Land, the place where the Shehina, G-d's most palpable presence rests, especially at the Holy Wall in Jerusalem's Old City. I go to the Wall a lot, every day for a while. I need all the help I can get.

In time, my prayers are answered. I find another Anglo—that is the local slang for native English speakers. We marry and, to my unbelievable delight, I become a mother.

When my daughter Shira is born we receive a gift—*Goodnight Moon* by Margaret Wise Brown. Every night I read it to her as I rock her to sleep. Her first book in English.

Twenty months later, I give birth again, this time to a son. I buy a bulky double stroller and push my two babies round our neighborhood, chattering to them in English— "this is the bird, this is the bush, this is the tree"… my boy and my girl.

I want my children to speak English, to be American. As soon as I can, I take them to the American consulate in East Jerusalem and register them as citizens. I don't care much about fitting in, becoming Israeli. In the suburban Anglo ghetto where I live, I sometimes forget that I'm in Israel at all. Most of my neighbors come from Teaneck, New Jersey, and our Brooklyn-born Rabbi gives his Sabbath morning sermon in English.

Like most my neighbors, every year, I fly "home" to visit loved ones and replenish my wardrobe at Talbots and the Gap, my library at Barnes and Noble even my medicine chest at Duane Reade. I come back with suitcases bulging with Dr. Seuss books, Tom's toothpaste, extra-strength Tylenol and Aveeno face cream, none of which are sold in Israel.

I don't make friends with Israelis. I don't think I really like them. When I do brush against them, on buses, in stores, at the playground, I find them brash, abrasive, unashamed to ask how old you are and how much you paid for your house.

I expect my children to be like me—Jewish enough to want to live in the Holy Land, but American enough to appreciate a bagel with cream cheese and lox and a fresh copy of the Sunday *New York Times*.

I have friends with kids like this, cultural chameleons who slip effortlessly between the two tongues that start on opposite sides of the page. It seems so natural, almost like walking or breathing, but it's not.

"Keeping up the English takes work," my best friend Dina warns me. I don't quite understand until one hot afternoon when I see what she means. Her son has just come home from soccer practice and requests a drink.

"Not until you ask in English," she says. He stands there panting, sweat rolling off his brow, and I wonder whether Dina is being unnecessarily cruel.

After several long minutes of haggling and whining, the boy switches tongues and Dina hands him a Coke.

But then I have other friends. Susie, whose kids speak an English that sounds like a bad imitation of Yiddish whirred through the food processor and Sara whose kids speak no English at all.

But Sara is married to a Sabra, a native Israeli who speaks to the kids in Hebrew, and Susie lives in poverty, without funds for English books, CDs, trips to the US.

As I'm neither married to an Israeli or poor, I am confident that I will succeed. Everyone tells me that children have brains like sponges just waiting to soak up languages. "Look at Europe where everyone speaks two or three languages," they all say. I want to believe this but I know better.

Nem tyudums magyarul. I don't speak Hungarian. Ironically that is one of the few full sentences I can say in my parents' mother tongue. I could have picked up more, even signed on for Hungarian as a language elective in college but I never wanted to.

Growing up, I knew kids who spoke the language, but not too many—Leslie Schreiber, a pudgy boy from a broken home whose mother taught him, and my weird cousin Ted, who turned out to be schizophrenic. My parents were disgusted by their fluency. "Why?" I remember my father asking. "Why does an American child need to know that?"

I heartily agree. English is enough. The perfect American English, that bubbles up from my throat like water from an underground spring. I love it, its cadences, its poetry, its literature—J.D. Salinger and Sylvia Plath, Bob Dylan and Paul Simon and Joni Mitchell and Suzanne Vega and Carole King.

I work hard to give my children English. I seek out English-speaking playgroups, nursery schools, summer camps, take them to English language story hour at our local library. There will be enough time to learn Hebrew later, from the school, from the street, from the air.

Then one day three months before my son's fourth birthday, Debbie, the teacher at his English-speaking nursery school pulls me off to the side.

"Michael isn't talking like the other kids," she whispers.

My heart is fluttering as if a pigeon has climbed into my chest.

What is wrong with my son? Why is Debbie the first to notice and not me?

At home, I repeat Debbie's words to my husband.

"Where did she get her PhD?" he asks. Mikey sounds fine to me."

"Let's play it safe," I say. I make an appointment with a speech pathologist, a Hunter College grad from the Bronx.

Clare wears a small crocheted hat over her graying hair. She leads Michael and me into her office through her backyard. Michael notices the lemon tree with large ripe lemons hanging from its branches.

"If you're good," Clare tells Michael, "I'll let you take one home." Amazingly, that is enough to get him through ninety minutes of testing.

While Michael and Clare wade through hundreds of flashcards and questions, I sit outside in Clare's living room-cum-waiting room nervously.

What are they doing in there? I can hardly hear Michael. His voice sounds too low, as if he's whispering. He must be afraid, I think; he always lowers his voice when he's afraid.

Through the thin door I hear them: Clare pointing to pictures, Michael struggling to identify them.

"Something Mommy uses on the fire to cook," I hear him mumble.

"Cook what?" she asks.

"Noodles."

"Oh, you mean a pot?" says Clare.

"Yes," I hear Michael answer.

A pot. My own son can't think of the word "pot." I bury my face in my hands and weep.

A week later I'm back at Clare's office, this time together with my husband, to hear the results.

Clare sits across from us in a swivel chair. My husband and I sit together opposite her in a battered love seat. Clare hunches forward, making sure that we hear every word she says.

"Your son has no real mother tongue."

No mother tongue. That sounds terrible, like there is something the matter with Michael's brain. I imagine a broken machine, like a telephone or a computer with the circuits pulled out.

Clare doesn't explain. Instead she goes for the solution which, like the lemons on her tree, is sour, hard to swallow.

"Choose one language for him and stick to it," she tells us. "Since you are living in Israel that language should be Hebrew."

Hebrew? I can hardly believe it. I know a few Americans who speak Hebrew at home, but they are fanatics, West Bank settlers, diehard Zionists, not people like me. I'm an American, and so is my son. How can I raise him without English? What will become of my polished, bilingual dream child?

"You want him to have a language don't you?" Clare asks somewhat menacingly.

Yes, we nod both of us feeling a little dazed.

"C'mon," my husband says. "It's not as if he's got cancer or something."

Unlike some of our friends, I can actually read, write, and speak Hebrew reasonably well, and so can my husband. He speaks it at work, but the only people I regularly speak Hebrew with are bank clerks, taxi drivers, and my cleaning lady.

From Clare's office we head to a Hebrew book store where I select my first Hebrew children's book—an old favorite, *Hazachal Haraev*, Eric Carle's *The Very Hungry Caterpillar* in Hebrew with the same leaf with the hole punched through but...

Zachal? What is that? A caterpillar, I guess. I see that Michael is not the only one with gaps in his Hebrew vocabulary.

Now Michael will be my Hebrew conversation partner, an at home *ulpan*.

I find a way to parent in two languages. At Shira's bedtime I read to her from *Stuart Little* and *All of a Kind Family*. Once a week a tutor visits the house to teach her to read and write in my mother tongue.

One day, when he's about eight, I ask the tutor if she could teach Michael, too. I want him to know English. I promised myself that my kids would speak English. She agrees, but after one session she quits. "He's just not ready. It's too much. Wait," she tells me.

Ironically, the person is my life most bothered by our new language regimen is my mother. "How will Michael get by in life?" she constantly asks. To her, English means safety, security, the almighty dollar, life. She also worries about being cut off from her grandchildren, stuck as I was for so long on the wrong side of a language chasm.

Sometimes I wonder about the language switch; whether it has done any of us any good. Even with the extra practice my Hebrew is still nothing to write home about. I wonder if I'm a lousy role model for my kids. It isn't just my American accent, which sounds like a Pontiac body wrapped round a Fiat motor, but my tendency to forget words or just not know them at all.

Vegetable peeler, (is that a *mikalef* or a *kalfan*) or colander (*mesanen* or *mesanenet*) or potato masher (*mauch*?). I fake it. Not the potato masher, but the instrument that turns boiled potatoes into puree. Not the sailor, but the soldier who fights at sea .

I even do what the speech therapist said never to do— I mix both languages. Baby carriage turns into *agala*. The corner grocery store is a *makolet*, a backpack, a *tik*, but other words remain forever in English, like iPod or toaster or freezer.

Sometimes I hear Michael and my younger children copying my mistakes.

I feel like I did when I was a child, that our communication is stuck on the simplest of levels.

"How was your day?" I ask Michael when he comes home from school.

"Okay," is always the answer. Never a story, joke, an anecdote for us to savor together.

Once in a while, I journey into my past to share myself with my son. With Michael it isn't dangerous, as it was with my parents for whom a simple question like, "Who was your best friend growing up?" could end with tears.

I tell Michael about my crazy childhood friend Susie

who once bought a set of gold-plated jacks at Brentanos just so that we could play, about winning a bubble gum blowing contest at a New York City street fair. But he doesn't get it.

Michael's never played jacks—no Israeli child plays that game. He's never been to a street fair—they don't have them here—and Brentanos, well, that venerable store has been gone for decades.

After Michael, I give birth to five more boys born in neat two year intervals and I stop travelling to the US. It's too hard and too expensive.

By now Hebrew has invaded our home. It's no longer part of the outside world, but it's inside now, part of us.

During these years, so many things happen, unbelievable things which make it impossible to pretend I'm living in the Middle Eastern part of Teaneck, New Jersey.

First, the Gulf War, waking up to the sound of sirens in the middle of the night, wondering if I am an in the middle of a chemical attack.

And after that, the second intifada. Days and months of listening to the radio and fighting back tears. The daughter of a friend blown up in a Jerusalem pizza shop. Her two older brothers, themselves only teenagers, go to the morgue to identify the body, "to spare their parents that much extra pain."

During the second intifada, and after that the second Lebanon war, I become addicted to the news, catching news flashes in Hebrew on the half hour. I care very deeply. These are not just abstract "Israelis" these are my people whose blood is being spilled, whether or not I know them personally. Their pain is my pain.

When overseas visitors comment on how my sons are "so Israeli," I feel good. Being Israeli has become something positive and strong. I feel proud of my people, the Chassidic rescue crews, who show up after each bombing with their garbage bags and scraping tools to wipe every last drop of blood and strewn body part from the pavement and bring it to proper Jewish burial. I feel proud of the rest of us, that we don't all have a collective nervous breakdown, that we find the strength to live and love even with a constant backdrop of terrible events.

Of course, sometimes, I still feel the outsider, like yesterday when my eight-year-old son came in boasting of a victory in *adjouim,* a tiddly winks-style game played with dried out apricot pits. As he tried explaining the rules, I drew a complete blank. I could see he was frustrated at a mom who couldn't even make sense of a kid's game. I wondered if he sometimes wished he had another mother, a Sabra, a native Israeli.

Last summer I took my sons to New York. For the first time they realized that not everybody speaks Hebrew. Michael, who is now seventeen, has begun teaching himself English from a workbook, and Joel, my second son, now speaks to me in English.

I loaded up on flash cards and phonics books to teach my younger sons English as a second language, not a mother tongue. I did promise myself that my kids would speak both languages.

It's Friday night again and this time it's my husband

who is ladling out the chicken soup. Once again, I'm surrounded by people speaking a foreign language, a language that is not mine. But then I do a double take. Hebrew is not Hungarian. Hebrew is my language, the language of my people, my prayers, the language of my soul.

The incredible thing about living here is the sparks of holiness that are everywhere. This is a country where *neshama*, or soul, is a term of endearment and a child's answer to the question "How are you?" is "Thank the Lord."

I am still in love with English, its rich vocabulary, its wonderful literature. I'd love for my kids to speak it really well, like I do, but it hasn't happened, not yet. Something else has happened instead.

My sons have become Sabras, real native Israelis. Sadly some of these bilingual chameleons have not fared so well. Shira now lives in New York City, not quite American and not quite Israeli, and two of Dina's kids have left Israel; one of them abandoning Judaism.

I'm not suggesting that being monolingual assures one's children a solid identity, but at least some of my family has stumbled upon a chance to let Israel sink in a little deeper and I'm glad for it.

A Hundred Years at Fifteen
by Xujun Eberlein

1.

My grandfather picks up a bamboo pole used to herd ducks, and chases my grandma across the yard in front of their thatch house. Crunching under her feet are the pale-yellow shells of harvested rapeseed spread under the sun to dry. "You unworthy hen who doesn't lay eggs!" he shouts, swinging the pole. "You ugly big foot!" he curses, baring his opium-yellowed teeth. But his pole can't reach its target. Grandma's wide bare feet trot too fast.

At fifteen, Grandma has two intolerable faults: she has yet to bear a baby, a full two years after her marriage as a child bride, and she has the biggest feet among the village women. Her feet were bound when she was six, the age she began her peasant duties, but every morning in the field she would cut the cloth bindings with her sickle, until her mother gave up rebinding them in the evening.

Grandma is not ashamed of her feet. They enable her, and she works faster than anyone in the village. But the image of a hen not laying eggs hurts. She wipes her tears with callused palms, and goes to the fields her husband's family rents from the landlord, to tend the corn, yam, potato, wheat, sorghum and opium. At one point she throws down her hoe and runs to a Guanyin temple. She does not have money to buy incense so she just kneels down to kowtow many times, her forehead punching the dirt ground. "Fertility Guanyin, Buddha of infinite compassion and mercy, please give me many children!"

That was the early summer of 1908, three years before the last dynasty in China ended, and Grandma lived in a poor rural area of the Zhong County on the upper Yangtze River, far away from the emperor. In time, Grandma would give birth to thirteen children, most born in the field while she worked alone. She cut the babies' umbilical cords with her plant-stained sickle. Twelve of the babies, the brothers and sisters of my mother, uncles and aunts of mine, did not survive disease and hunger to see their first birthday.

Only my mother was exempt.

2.

At fifteen, my mother escapes from an arranged marriage. The arrangement was made three years before, over a table of engagement wine, by a matchmaker and the heads of two families. Her fiancé, the son of a wine yeast producer surnamed Qin, is two years older than she and is about to become an apprentice at a Chinese herb medicine store in the county. His parents request a formal wedding before his departure.

My mother has never met the Qin family's son, nor is she interested. "I don't want to marry," she tells Grandma, "I don't want to marry a medicine apprentice in the mountains."

"What do you want to do?" Grandma asks.

"To study in high school, or go to the front to fight the war against the Japanese invaders," says my mother.

Financially supported by her teachers, she is about to graduate from the local middle school at the top of her class. Several of the teachers are exiles from Japanese-occupied areas in the north and they have opened her eyes to the bigger world.

Grandma, an illiterate peasant who has never left her village, does not know what the war front is or why the Japanese are in our country. She knows, though, that there is no high school in town and there are many good schools in the big city, Chongqing, three days away by ship, upstream on the Yangtze.

Grandma borrows a floral quilt and a cardboard suitcase from the landlord, and packs for her daughter. She carries the quilt on her shoulders and walks with my mother, her only child, her treasure and hope, for one and a half days along winding mountain paths. My fifteen-year-old mother carries the borrowed suitcase, sweat soaking her home-dyed cheongsam, light blue (or dark blue, the only two colors Grandma can afford). Sewn inside the seam of the cheongsam are a few small bills, travel money pooled by her teachers. Her new black cloth shoes, with thickly layered soles that took Grandma many nights to stitch together, sustain her feet through the long tramp. At the port of "Ghost City Fengdu," they meet my mother's cousin who is on his way back to his college in Chongqing. The two young people board a wooden sampan that takes them to a two-story passenger ship (there is no dock).

My mother waved goodbye to her mother, my grandma, on that summer day of 1945. The ship sailed for the big city Chongqing, where she would attend a government subsidized normal school, graduate, join the Communist underground and meet my father, a city orphan and fellow revolutionary. Together they risked their lives fighting for an "ideal society." A decade later, a rising Communist cadre in the New China, my mother gave birth to me, her third daughter.

3.

I enter Chongqing's 29th middle school at fifteen. I am late—we are all late, the schools were closed for several years since the Cultural Revolution began. We have some regular lessons, like Chinese, Math, and Physics, but more time is spent reading Party documents and newspapers. We are bored.

One day the boredom is interrupted. "Every student must come to school this evening. There will be a display of a negative example," the school's broadcast announces. Evening activities are rare, and we are excited.

"What is it about?" I ask a girl who always seems to know these things.

"They caught a 'Sis Wang'," she tells me in a mysterious tone.

I know "Sis Wang" is a dirty name for a teenage girl who does very bad things. What very bad things? I am not sure, and I am glad to have a chance to find out.

The evening comes, and we walk quietly in line into a classroom-turned-exhibit area. We slowly circle a table set in the middle of the room, in front of which a teenage girl stands, head lowered, face hidden behind dense, messy, long hair. A notebook lays open on the table beside a sign: "yellow diary." (In the lexicon of 1970 China, "yellow" means pornography, and no crime is more appalling than that.) These are the objects on display: a girl our age and her diary.

When it is my turn to approach the table, I stare at the faceless girl, wanting to see how she looks. Except for the long hair, she appears no different than us, wearing the same colorless long sleeve shirt, tightly buttoned. Perhaps sensing my wish, she tosses her head, clearing strands of hair from her cheeks. For a moment I see a pretty oval face with an indifferent expression, as if all of us, the viewers, are not of her species. I avert my eyes, looking down at the open page of the diary as a gust of wind chills the hot summer night. And the night is dark, the wind is sad; in a corner of a park, a lone girl waits for her love, and he has not come....

Before I can read more, I am pushed away by the students behind me. Everyone is eager to see the girl and her yellow diary, like watching an exotic animal newly arrived in the zoo.

It was not the words but the sensual image that had stayed with me. Her shame was startling, and her longing for love frightening. (At that time the word "love" was reserved for Chairman Mao and the Party.) I did not understand why those poetic lines in her diary were "yellow," and it did not seem I should ask my mother. For if I did, she would have spoken the same words as the school authority and the newspaper. Whether or not this "negative example" contributed to my retardedness in understanding sex, a dozen years later I remained a virgin.

Unintended, my waiting was ended by a young American who walked into the newly opened gate of China and, to the sound of Dvorak's Ninth Symphony, proposed.

4.

My American-born daughter turns fifteen in our suburban Boston home, far enough away from Iraq that the machine gun fire and bombings can't be heard. Among the birthday gifts she asks for—and gets—is an iPod Mini, a palm-size, olive green box that can store more than a thousand songs and costs two months of my sister's salary in China. In the news, the iPod is noted as the most popular present for American teenagers.

She also gets several boxes of Star Trek DVDs: The Original Series, The Next Generation, Voyager, and two movies. It is a thing that she and her dad share a prolonged enthusiasm for. Two years before, she watched an episode of Star Trek Enterprise on TV, and saw T'Pol eating carrots with a knife and a fork. "That is *so* cool," my daughter said. The next day she became a vegetarian. But there weren't many vegetables that she liked. A year later she was diagnosed with anemia and it scared me to death. After her recovery, being a vegetarian becomes her cause.

Despite the birthday presents, she is all gloomy. "School sucks," she frets—she has to do homework (instead of spending time on Instant Messenger). This complaint is a motto among her high school friends. Despite her status as an honor student, schooling seems the greatest suffering in her life. I tell her my desperation—and her grandma's—for education; she sees her Chinese ancestors as losers. "You get to be President of America not knowing how to spell," she says. Whether she is sarcastic or not is anyone's guess.

She goes to an evening party wearing camo pants—another birthday gift. Attending the party are five girls and two boys, half of them fellow vegetarians. One boy's mother drops him off at the host girl's door and reminds him to check in.

The boy calls his mom at about 10:00pm. When he dials, my daughter is sitting on his lap (because he liked her camo pants).

"What's up?" his mother asks on the phone.

"Nothing. Talking."

My daughter tickles his stomach and he yelps.

"Remember to use a condom," the mother jokes, hanging up as laughter erupts in the room.

My daughter is still chuckling when she tells us this in the car.

"You were sitting on his lap?" I say, in a tone I hope is composed.

"Oh c'mon, Mom. It's not like everyone else doesn't already have a boyfriend."

Her dad rolls the steering wheel and I sway toward the passenger window clouded by the night fog. Without looking I know he is smiling in the dark. My husband is American. Americans take everything lightly.

"I didn't even know what animal a boyfriend was when I was fifteen," I say.

My daughter giggles, "Don't be upset, Mom. He's gay."

I wait, but her dad says nothing. He makes another turn, and I tilt to the right. Outside the window is now milky and opaque. I can't make out the road. What turn did we make last time? Surely we're not going in circles. Are we?

"Jeez, Dad, do you have to drive so slow?" my daughter says. "Next year, I drive."

Adapting Back Home
by Andrea Martins

"Off you go, run around, enjoy yourselves," I said, reveling in a gorgeous, sunny day at the park with the ocean sparkling in the background.

My two-and-a-half-year-old daughter ran full steam ahead—anxious to explore. My four-year-old son, however, ran only a few steps, stopped, looked around puzzled as to why I was not following him, as I had always done in security-conscious Mexico City, and asked, "You mean we can run *anywhere*?"

It was at that very moment, in our first week back in Australia, that it hit me: while repatriation for me was probably going to be more like switching hats—back to what I had known before—life in Australia was going to be a whole new learning experience for our Australian-born children who had never known what it was like to really *live* in Australia.

This was reiterated when my son started introducing himself that day to everyone in the playground.

"Hello, I'm Bailey. I'm from Australia. Where are you from?"

Needless to say, in a park full of Australians, my son innocently became the subject of great bemusement.

"Don't worry," chimed in a well-meaning member of our extended family. "Children learn quickly. They will adapt faster than you think and they will soon forget what they did and where they lived before."

"But I don't want them to forget," I thought to myself. "Why would I want them to forget the formative years of their lives, their international friends, their Spanish language skills, the food, our travel and our experiences?"

Little did I know just how quickly my children would learn and *adapt*. Two weeks into our arrival home, my son spoke the words I dreaded most: "Stop reading it in Spanish, Mum. Just read it normal." Newsflash Mum, no one here speaks anything other than English, so only read it in English.

My heart sank. Was this going to be the beginning of the end? I wondered, knowing how difficult learning a new language was as an adult and praying that our children would somehow retain their bilingual skills. How could they be ready to ditch speaking Spanish, after only two weeks back in Australia?

"Come on darling," I replied calmly, quelling the mix of emotions beneath my skin. "I love hearing it in Spanish and it would be great if you and Jasmine practiced your Spanish." I soldiered on with my plan to read the book in both languages, as we had always done.

"No, Mum. No," he replied, cheered on by his sister, who hated the thought of being left out.

It did not matter how many times I tried after that; my children were apparently *adapting*, Australian-style. I didn't like it, but I couldn't stop it. I did manage, however, to sneak a dozen or so Spanish words into our family's daily vocabulary. The words themselves were not important; what mattered was the satisfaction I derived from hearing them spoken each day. To me, this was at least some kind of recognition of the past—of where we were and who we used to be.

At the same time, the daily pleads of: "Mum, when can we go back and visit Alesi, Gaby, Quique, Amani and all of our friends in Mexico?" were gradually beginning to fade. It was not long before the question was asked only once a week, then once a month, and now, eighteen months on, it is rarely asked at all.

Instead, every night in our bedtime song, we sing the names of all of the children's old friends from abroad. If I am honest, I am sure that the children do not really remember their old friends and they just sing with me because I'm the one who made up the song. We sing it anyway. It makes me happy.

In the absence of bilingual skills and international friends, I have struggled with how else I can keep our international experience in our children's consciousness. I borrow books from the library and read to my children about people living in different cultures. I engage the kids in discussions around our large world map. I encourage them to taste foods from different countries and take the opportunity to explain to them snippets of information about that country and its people. I keep an eye out for people wearing different clothing and take each opportunity to explain to my children about the country of the unsuspecting passers-by. All the while, I find myself trying to weave our children's international experience into our discussions in the hope that they will retain at least some sense of their previous identity.

To my great delight, Australian shops now sell piñatas, papier mâché shapes, typically themed with famous children's characters, which you put candies in for the children at birthday parties. I buy these piñatas in an attempt to hold on to some legacy of Mexico in our birthday celebrations. However, the piñatas here are very small and are all pull-string, rather than the have-a-great-time-by-hitting-with-a-bat-with-all-of-your-strength-while-singing-the-traditional-Mexican-piñata-song type. My kids love both. But to me, the piñatas in Australia are just not the same.

My new friends here are very nice. They all seem to be either Australians or soon-to-be-Australians, immigrating typically from England, South Africa or the United States. But none of them seem to live in that highly-mobile state of mind that characterizes most expatriates that I know, and which I confess, is a little addictive.

My immigrant friends here know exactly what it is like to take their children from one culture and re-plant them in another. However, unlike me, they appear okay with their children giving up what they left behind. They encourage their children to embrace everything Australian, as soon as possible.

I want my kids to adapt and fit in… but not completely. I want them to remember their past identity and experiences; blend those with the here and now; and leave room for the possibility that our family might move abroad again in the future. I want my kids to be internationals: multi-lingual, multi-talented, and multi-dimensional. I want my kids to be different.

Maybe that is the problem.

As a repatriate who struggles with the notion of being stuck in one location, who regularly yearns to be overseas again and who, despite a large network of wonderful new friends, feels like she does not completely fit in, I look at my happy, healthy, well-adjusted children who have bloomed in their new lives back home and I think of the irony: it is me, the Australian-born, Australian-raised one, who has not adapted. I am the one that does not seem to have learned very well.

Maybe I need to file my past memories away in a sacred box of treasures that is closed more than it is opened, live life more in the present, take more time here to enjoy those around me, and let the future work itself out—free from my expectations of what it *should* be.

As my son would say, "We're in Australia now, Mum."

Perhaps it is my children who have had it right all along.

The View from the Outside
by Marie Lamba

"I feel like I don't belong. Like some fraud. I mean, where am I supposed to fit in?"

I opened my mouth to answer, but didn't know quite what to say. My eldest daughter Adria, a senior in high school, had always been so self-assured. Half Asian-Indian and half Italian-American, she never once had expressed any conflict over her mixed heritage. Now she was eighteen and going off to spend three days at the Multicultural Scholars Weekend. It was being held at the university where she was accepted for the following year.

"I mean, it's not as if I really am like any of them," she was saying.

"It's not?" I said, trying hard not to put words in her mouth.

"No," she said after a moment of silence. "It's not like I'm black or Asian or Latino or anything. Maybe I shouldn't go."

She felt like a true outsider. And at that moment, I felt like I had somehow failed both of my daughters. Adria and Cari (who is 13) were raised in the suburbs of Pennsylvania far from any Indian relatives. But what more could I have done? I'm not the Indian one in the mix. I'm the Italian-American Jersey girl. So I shared with them my Italian cooking, and my love of reading, I took them to CCD classes so they could become confirmed Catholics, saw that they participated in Girl Scouts, and drove them to music lessons. In short, I passed on to them what I had grown up with. What did I know about the Indian culture? Nothing until I'd met my husband. What did I know about raising multicultural kids? Absolutely nothing at all!

Over the years, my husband did what he could to share his culture with the girls. When they were little he read them Panchantra and Jataka Tales. From time to time he'd cook curries or purchase cases of ripe mangoes and boxes of sticky Indian sweets. He even showed them the occasional Bollywood movie just for laughs. But he never taught them any Punjabi beyond counting to ten. Of course, if I were Indian, we'd have been speaking this all the time at home, and the girls would have naturally picked it up...

Adria and Cari *look* Indian, though perhaps more fair-skinned than most. They've also been mistaken for Latino, and for Native American. One thing's for sure, they look different from me. Especially near the end of the summer when their skin becomes a deep coffee tone, and I remain, well, milky. Now that they are growing into mature young women, when we are out together people are confused by our relationship to each other. Adria and I were recently stopped at a museum where we had a family membership. The woman at the door didn't believe Adria was my daughter, and wanted to charge her a separate fee for getting in.

So the girls look exotic, but are they? Aren't they just typical American teens? As my children are becoming young women and going off on their own, I guess they will be searching more and more for their place in the world. Where will they fit in? Will they always feel like outsiders?

I know a bit about being an outsider. Marrying outside my culture threw me into a foreign world I knew nothing about. Suddenly I was visiting India and surrounded by an extended family who spoke in heavily accented English, except for when they would break into Punjabi with each other, which they often did. Then I'd find myself smiling and nodding, pretending that I understood, even though I didn't have a clue.

We again visited India when Adria was three, then took both the girls when Cari was five and Adria was ten. Never were they more immersed in Indian culture. Their clothing and mannerisms set them apart from the locals, but they were able to hang out with their cousins, and fly kites on the roof, and explore the ancient temples, and even ride an elephant up to a desert palace. It wasn't like coming home, it was more like an incredibly exciting adventure. And often they were unsure and uncomfortable with some of the differences. The lack of personal space. The foreign language. The unrecognizable food. The frightening attention from street beggars.

Then they would slip their hands in mine for reassurance. I would smile, and we'd talk about what was strange to us, what was fascinating, what was hilarious. My girls and I were outsiders together, and it was a comfort to me as well.

Whenever Indian relatives came to visit us in the US, we again experienced a bit of this feeling. Our familiar suburban house seemed to change. Aunties started chop-chopping onions in the kitchen, and cumin seeds started smoking on the grill. Turbaned uncles sat in chairs sipping tea and stroking their moustaches. Punjabi chatter flew about the room. The girls dressed more conservatively. They spoke in formal tones. And they hung around me more than usual. We were the outsiders together again, until they felt comfortable enough with the family members to sit with, and eventually interact with them.

As they've become older, I've noticed this change dramatically. The girls now feel so comfortable with whoever visits, they immediately connect with them, acting like they would on any other day.

Last summer we went to a nephew's wedding. It was completely traditional, seemingly straight off the streets of New Delhi (even though it was actually in Memphis, Tennessee). And while I was just a guest, my daughters had an important role to play. Since my nephew had no sisters, the girls were taking on that job, and had to participate in countless little rituals over a few days. The culmination, of course, was on the wedding day itself.

The groom, with golden tinsel hanging from his turban and concealing his face, sat atop a white horse (yes, a real horse) in the Temple parking lot. Raucous Bollywood music blasted from someone's car speakers. Indians dressed in rich silks and dazzling traditional finery surrounded the horse, and beside the horse were my two daughters, looking as Indian as can be. Their hands were stained with customary henna patterns, and they clapped along, laughing.

There were lots of family members that I had known from over the years, and many more relatives from the groom's other side of the family who we'd never met before.

Many had flown in from India just for this occasion. I stood on the outside of the crowd, but my girls were in the middle of the circle, surrounded by tradition and family and love. They had become the insiders. They didn't need my reassurance anymore.

The girls were handed tinsel and people started telling them what to do with it. Telling them in *Punjabi*. Adria looked confused. Folks started to become impatient, waving their hands at them, wondering why these Indian girls didn't follow simple directions. Voices became raised. The girls stared at each other, and for a moment it seemed as if Cari might burst into tears.

What could I do to help? I couldn't translate. I didn't know the rituals, either. But they clearly needed me. I was about to push through the crowd and come to the rescue, shouting, "They aren't Indian. They don't speak Punjabi. Go easy on them!"

Before I could even take a step forward, someone took the tinsel from their hands, and tied it onto the horse's halter. "There!" he said.

Everyone laughed, and so did my girls. They were handed more tinsel and decorated the horse with it to everyone's satisfaction. Then they were gone.

I craned my neck to see where they'd went to, only to find them by my side, slipping their arms through mine, and observing. It seems they were happy to have been the insiders for a while, but just as happy to be the outsiders.

So perhaps raising biracial daughters is about showing them how to cope on both the inside and the outside of their respective cultures, with humor and curiosity and confidence.

Adria did go on that Multicultural Scholar's Weekend. When she got there, she was happy to find a number of biracial kids, including a tall blond-haired blue-eyed boy from Mexico. But the best part was how she instantly floated among the various ethnic groups, making friends with people of all different backgrounds. And when she got home, I asked her, "So, where did you fit in?"

"Everywhere, Mom. Everywhere."

ABOUT THE CONTRIBUTORS

Katherine Barrett is an at-home mother of three preschoolers—all boys, all boisterous and all beautiful. In her infrequent stretches of quiet time she writes, and in a former life she was a relatively together academic. They're Canadian but are currently living in the Western Cape in South Africa. She has recently published in *Mom Writer's Literary Magazine* and blogs at twinutero.org and motherverse.com.

Michele Corkery is a writer/communications professional who lives with her visual-artist husband and daughter in a work/live artist loft in Boston, MA. She has a Bachelor's from Bates College and a MFA in Creative Writing from Emerson College. Her writing has been published in literary journals and local newspapers.

Xujun Eberlein grew up in Chongqing, China, moved to the United States in 1988, and holds a PhD from M.I.T. Author of the award-winning short story collection, *Apologies Forthcoming* (Livingston Press), she lives with her husband and daughter in Wayland, Massachusetts. "One Hundred Years at Fifteen" was originally published in *Post Road.*

Anjali Enjeti-Sydow is a recovering attorney living near Atlanta with her husband and three daughters, Mira, Leela and Siri. She has written for several print and online parenting publications, Dot Moms, and is the author of the column "Mixing It Up" at mamazine.com, where her essay first appeared in slightly different form.

Saffia Farr is the author of *Revolution Baby: Motherhood and Anarchy in Kyrgyzstan,* an account of her three years in the former Soviet republic. She maintains a website at www.saffiafarr.com.

Violeta Garcia-Mendoza is a Spanish-American poet, writer, and teacher. Her poetry has appeared in a variety of literary venues, including *Cicada, Tattoo Highway,* and *The Pittsburgh Post-Gazette,* and her prose appears regularly in her monthly "Multi-Culti Mami" column at *Literary Mama.* Violeta makes her multi-culti home in Pennsylvania, with her American husband, Guatemalan-born children, and Welsh Corgi dogs. For more information, please visit her website: www.TurnPeoplePurple.com.

A displaced Texan by choice, **Kathy Hamilton**'s first visit to Turkey was in 1981, on the heels of a military coup. In spite of the short-term civil unrest, she continued to return for vacations until finally succumbing to the lure of Istanbul and moving permanently to Istanbul in 1998. Her work as a correspondent for one of the national newspapers covers expat lifestyles, culture, food and off the beaten track historic sites. She also writes for *Hali* magazine on the antique carpet business in Turkey and the US. Her writing is included in the international best-selling anthology *Tales From the Expat Harem; Mexico: A Love Story* and *A Woman's World Again.*

Corey Heller is the founder of the Bilingual/Bicultural Family Network (www.biculturalfamily.org) and the Editor-in-Chief of *Multilingual Living Magazine,* a digital publication dedicated to families around the world raising children in more than one language and culture. She lives in Seattle with her German husband and three children ages 3, 5 and 6. You can reach her at corey@biculturalfamily.org or visit her blog at anamerican-betweenworlds.blogspot.com.

Juli Herman lives in Ohio with her husband and four children. While her husband strives to finish graduate school, she homeschools her children, dives into writing, and dabbles in various projects.

Rose Kent lives in upstate New York. Her first children's novel *Kimchi & Calamari* (HarperCollins, 2007) is a recommended selection by The Anti-Defamation League and is on the state reading lists in Florida and Wisconsin. Visit her at www.RoseKent.com.

Marie Lamba is author of the humorous young adult novel *What I Meant...* (Random House, 2008), which features a biracial heroine. She is also the parent of two biracial children, and frequently speaks about the need for multiracial characters in fiction. You can visit her at www.marielamba.com.

Stacy M. Lewis lives in Seattle with her husband and their two sons, who are now five and two. "Ghost Stories" originally appeared in *Brain, Child* magazine. Stacy blogs at www.mama-om.com.

Devorah Lifshutz is the pen name for a born and bred New Yorker now living in Israel. Lifshutz is a freelance writer and sometimes writing teacher whose work including articles, short stories personal essays and poetry appeared in American and Israeli newspapers, books and magazines. Lifshutz writes to keep sane. Most of the time she's a full time, stay at home Mom. The alias is intended to protect the privacy of her loved ones.

Leza Lowitz is an award-winning writer, editor, screenwriter and co-translator. Her work has appeared in hundreds of literary journals and anthologies, and she has published over 15 books, including *Yoga Poems: Lines to Unfold By* and *Green Tea to Go: Short Stories from Tokyo*. Her awards include the PEN Josephine Miles Award, a PEN Syndicated Fiction Award, grants from the NEA and NEH, and the Japan-U.S. Friendship Commission Award for the translation of Japanese literature from Columbia University. She lives in Tokyo where she owns the popular Sun and Moon Yoga studio. She can be reached at www.lezalowitz.com or www.redroom.com.

Kate MacVean lives in Spain with her husband and their three sons. For two years she wrote a column, "Mothering Abroad," for the online journal *Literary Mama*, and her poetry has been published in *Tattoo Highway*. She continues to try to expand her kids' taste horizons, with varying degrees of success. She also reports that after writing this essay, she tried some of the leaner bits of the lamb roast at the village fiestas, and next year may even have a full portion.

Andrea Martins is the Co-Founder and Director of ExpatWomen.com—a global resource site designed to help all women, of all nationalities, living overseas. www.ExpatWomen.com

Susannah Elisabeth Pabot holds an MA in children's literature. She worked as a London-based journalist specializing in the children's book market before moving to Paris, where she now lives with her French husband and three-year-old daughter. Susannah's writing has appeared in numerous trade magazines, including *The Bookseller* and *The Children's*

Bookseller, and in *Literary Mama,* and is forthcoming in an academic anthology. She is currently working on her first short story collection.

Dee Thompson is a writer and lives with her children in Atlanta, Georgia. Her blog is called The Crab Chronicles, http://deescribbler.typepad.com/my_weblog/ and her book is called *Adopting Alesia: My Crusade for My Russian Daughter.*

Holly Thompson is the author of the novel *Ash* (Stone Bridge Press), set in Kyoto and Kagoshima, and the picture book *The Wakame Gatherers* (Shen's Books). She is Regional Advisor of SCBWI Tokyo and teaches poetry and fiction writing at Yokohama City University.

Angela Turzynski-Azimi was born and bred in the north of England. She has lived and worked in various parts of England, as well as Wales, Switzerland, Japan and Australia. A graduate of the University of London (S.O.A.S.), she currently lives in Yokohama, Japan, with her husband and son, where she works as a freelance translator. Her published translations include *Kendo: The Definitive Guide,* published by Kodansha International. She has also taught at universities in Japan and Australia.

CPSIA information can be obtained
at www.ICGtesting.com
Printed in the USA
LVHW011621121022
730562LV00003B/380

9 781932 279337